Translating and Interpreting Justice in a Postmonolingual Age

Edited by

Esther Monzó-Nebot
Universitat Jaume I, Spain
&
Juan Jiménez-Salcedo
Universidad Pablo de Olavide, Spain

Series in Language and Linguistics

Copyright © 2019 Vernon Press, an imprint of Vernon Art and Science Inc, on behalf of the author.

All rights reserved. No part of this publication may be reproduced, stored in a retrieval system, or transmitted in any form or by any means, electronic, mechanical, photocopying, recording, or otherwise, without the prior permission of Vernon Art and Science Inc.

www.vernonpress.com

In the Americas:
Vernon Press
1000 N West Street,
Suite 1200, Wilmington,
Delaware 19801
United States

In the rest of the world:
Vernon Press
C/Sancti Espiritu 17,
Malaga, 29006
Spain

Series in Language and Linguistics

Library of Congress Control Number: 2017964068

ISBN: 978-1-62273-689-8

Also available:

Hardback: 978-1-62273-312-5

E-book: 978-1-62273-523-5

Product and company names mentioned in this work are the trademarks of their respective owners. While every care has been taken in preparing this work, neither the authors nor Vernon Art and Science Inc. may be held responsible for any loss or damage caused or alleged to be caused directly or indirectly by the information contained in it.

Every effort has been made to trace all copyright holders, but if any have been inadvertently overlooked the puwill be pleased to include any necessary credits in any subsequent reprint or edition.

Table of Contents

Chapter 1	Introduction. Translation and postmonolingualism	1
Chapter 2	Translators and interpreters as agents of diversity. Managing myths and pursuing justice in postmonolingual societies	9
Chapter 3	Unveiling and redressing inequality dynamics in legal and institutional translation: from symbolic violence to symbolic recognition	35
Chapter 4	Translating and interpreting cultures. Discussing translation and interpreting ethics in a postmonolingual age	61
Chapter 5	Translation and climate justice: Minority perspectives	77
Chapter 6	The role of indigenous interpreters in the Peruvian intercultural, bilingual justice system	91
Chapter 7	Translation and interpreting policies in China: Ethnic linguistic minorities in the judicial system	111
Chapter 8	The asymmetry of Canada's language policy regarding access to justice: a model for managing postmonolingualism	127
List of contributors		*141*
Index		*145*

Chapter 1

Introduction.
Translation and postmonolingualism

Esther Monzó-Nebot & Juan Jiménez-Salcedo

The evolution of our world has resulted in diverse social and political communities whose will to grow stronger together has nourished a shared culturally diverse present. International organizations and international cooperation have developed at a healthy pace over the last century and have brought about the most complex system of global organization to ever inhabit the planet. However, current demographic flows caused by political upheavals, war conflicts, climate change, and the demolition of boundaries in the labor market have increased the tempo of demographic changes at an unprecedented rate and have at times overwhelmed the capacity of international organizations and domestic systems to develop efficient social policies and to empower modern citizens to deal with an increasing diversity. Evidence-based approaches and strategies to refocus, streamline, repair and rebuild community policies are required to successfully cater to diversity in sustainable ways. Our social spaces have become a meeting point of a myriad of languages and cultures, whose diversity is only expected to increase (Cornelius and Rosenblum 2005), and personal histories of mobility and diaspora have multiplied, invigorating the complexities of both our identities and our possibilities.

These social changes have been mirrored by academic efforts to describe and explain the intricacy of current social and personal experiences. One of the tools developed to describe our present contexts is postmonolingualism. Based on Gogolin's ideas on multilingualism (1994), Yildiz coined the term in 2012 to defy the urge to cast unified linguistic systems onto identities that develop in liminal cultural spaces. Having just one mother tongue is no longer the norm. Feeling, thinking, and interacting following the logic of one culture can no longer be reasonably expected. And yet the impact of monolingualism on individuals' lives (Gogolin 2009) and cultural production and dissemination (Yildiz 2012) lingers on establishing *normality* – in a Foucaultian sense (see Foucault 1975) – as the only acceptable choice. For centuries, languages had been the backbones of political spaces and creative subjectivities. Languages are still used to identify cultures, grant nationalities and define the limits of authority. However, the 21st century is being defined by a normal coexistence of diverse languages, cultures and identities in shared physical and online spaces. Since the times where Sennett defined a city as a site where "strangers are likely to meet" (1978, p. 39), our experience with strangeness has only increased. Step by step, we are keeping up with an empirical world that urges us to challenge a monolingual spirit hindering our social, political, cultural, moral, and personal evolutions. Postmonolingualism allows us to question the moral and social authority derived from any particular language, nation, religion, cultural values, abilities, gender, or sexual orientation. A postmonolingual world thus demands key concepts such as justice, equality, freedom and democracy to be reexamined.

Coming from minoritized identities in an assimilationist State, the editors of this volume saw in postmonolingualism a tool for challenging heteronomous boundaries and authority policies. The Translation and Postmonolingualism (TRAP) research group, established at Universitat Jaume I, Spain, has taken upon the task of revealing monolingual paradigms in all areas of society and contesting their drive for normalization, from global to local societal efforts. In partnership with Linguapax International, TRAP acts as a hub for developing descriptive approaches, identifying actionable issues and providing policy recommendations to address the needs of our new complexities for diverse and super-diverse societies (Vertovec 2007) to thrive in a global environment striving for political recognition and contesting the populist majoritarianism (Grigoriadis 2018) that endangers the progress of just and plural societies.

Diversity is enshrined in a number of international instruments, such as the United Nations Sustainable Development Goals (UNGA 2015) or the Universal Declaration on Cultural Diversity (UNESCO 2001), as a value to be protected. Yet, the means to achieve mutual understanding in diverse populations and the sustainability of such understanding are overwhelmingly lacking in the formulation of the policy instruments leading international efforts. TRAP works on the conviction that recognition at a global level requires hard evidence of the traps posited by the monolingual design of policies impacting social cooperation, of the efficiencies of postmonolingualism in ensuring prosper intergroup relations and of the returns of proactive translation and interpreting policies in achieving sustainable diversity. Translation and interpreting are necessary means to ensure inclusive dialogue, enhance intercultural and intergroup understanding, inspire respect for difference, raise awareness as to the requirements of political recognition for all identities and lead the way towards effective social justice.

Justice is indeed a value at the core of this book and of TRAP's work. From differing perspectives, the contributions collected in this volume oppose majority as the source of legitimacy and see political recognition as the basis of any system truthfully concerned with democracy (Beetham 2017). Against the background of increasingly diverse societies, the path towards equal representation is by no means led by an easy track and needs to be firmly grounded in awareness and negotiation of differences. This negotiation is at the base of contractualist views on justice, which see justice as fairness and underscore the role of institutions in positive distribution to correct morally arbitrary inequalities (Rawls 1971), that is, the privilege with which specific genders, languages, religions, capacities, ethnic or family origins are born and allowed to develop in society. Social justice is thus understood as an institutionally led active process of reenfranchisement and, within this framework, translation and interpreting are processes ensuring that all individuals can first have a real option to participate in the political life to negotiate the social contract they will be bound by and, second, exercise their rights on equality with others without sacrificing their differences. It is translation and interpreting that can advance communication of and within diversity, by affording voices in languages that can be heard where they need to reach, but also by lending and investing in understanding between identities so that monolingual paradigms can be overwritten and diversity can be sustained.

As a defining feature of identity[1] and the vehicle for the naturalization of narratives constructing identities and intergroup relations, language is a cornerstone for our work. TRAP focuses on achieving social and political impact by creating knowledge on current contexts of diversity and on the problems derived from and created by monolingual approaches to social organization. Addressing the different situations of verbal and sign languages and exploring the possibilities of verbal and non-verbal linguistic uses, TRAP develops postmonolingual approaches and solutions to improve intergroup and intercultural relations emphasizing the merits of multicultural understanding in different settings.

Among such settings, educational institutions are at the basis of developing a sustainable understanding for future generations. TRAP's research in this area focuses on developing plurilingual competence in elementary and secondary school students through the integration of migrants' languages into school activities. The exposition to and explicitation of linguistic diversity contributes to the development of positive attitudes towards global and

---

[1] See Stokes (2017), where language is reported by a majority of citizens as the most prominent criterion in accepting immigrants.

multicultural environments and the active countering of intolerant narratives (and the myths and symbols enshrined in those narratives) by the students, who nurture positive views on diversity. The components of global (OECD 2016) and intercultural (Hammer 2015) competence are thus developed in youngsters within the framework of a postmonolingual society (Marzà and Ríos 2016).

A second area of research in the work of TRAP focuses on court and police settings. The processes where cognitive biases are activated in interaction are analyzed against the background of power imbalances that impact the ability of individuals to participate in communicative encounters. From the roles defined by deontological codes and uncritically accepted (by interpreters, police mediators or social workers) to the confirmation bias (Wason 1960; 1968) that discards information which may challenge intergroup and intercultural prejudices, or the impact of intragroup affinity and intergroup hostility on governance, communicative tools (including the explicitation of cultural knowledge and uses of nonverbal language) are exploited to level the ground and improve intergroup and intercultural understanding in mediated situations for interpreters, translators, educators, social workers, law-enforcement and judicial agents, especially focusing on minoritized languages and disprivileged groups (Monzó-Nebot and Jiménez-Salcedo 2017).

Following the first formulations of postmonolingualism, a third strand of research focuses on the translation of literary and audiovisual products where conflicts among monolingualisms are fictionalized and made visible, and where translators show a tendency to normalize, simplify and misrepresent identities (Molines Galarza 2017). The interaction between dominant and minoritized languages in literature relating multilingual experiences in Nazi concentration camps or the creation of new languages to allow identities to resist the disciplines marked by hegemonic sociocultural systems are brought in focus to disentangle the components of the postmonolingual condition.

This volume collects contributions from authors who conduct research within those areas and that encourage us to enjoy our postmonolingual condition while critically examining the restraints imposed by monolingualism. The present book is an attempt to offer a compendium of views on the theoretical approaches and practical applications of postmonolingual policies in modern societies. The contents are structured in two parts. The first four chapters develop four different conceptual approaches to postmonolingualism as a tool to manage social diversity. Those first four chapters share a process-oriented approach to ethically responding to social demands through translation and interpreting. The second part comprises three chapters where practical solutions implemented in multicultural contexts are examined from a postmonolingual mindset. Policies and efforts to foster social justice in postmonolingual societies through translation and interpreting are critically scrutinized, weaknesses and strengths are identified the lessons learned are further suggested as the basis for new initiatives that can enhance our experience of diversity.

After this introduction, translation and interpreting are contextualized in the times marked by diverse societies. In the first chapter, Esther Monzó-Nebot ("Translators and interpreters as agents of diversity. Managing myths and pursuing justice in postmonolingual societies") highlights how a proactive translation and interpreting policy can enrich intergroup understanding and foster the principles of democracy and social justice. The dominant policies on intergroup relations and ideas of social justice are examined against the background of modern diverse societies and the need for modern humans to face and understand difference. The psychosocial factors affecting intergroup relations and the need for translators and interpreters to develop a metacognitive awareness of biases and a critical stance on intergroup conflict are presented as crucial in understanding and managing otherness in intergroup communication. Monzó-Nebot's discussion of justice, diversity and translation highlights contributions that conceive of social justice as a process where the right of all identities to decide on our common future serves as the basis for understanding our differences.

Rosario Martín Ruano ("Unveiling and redressing inequality dynamics in legal and institutional translation: from symbolic violence to symbolic recognition") focuses on a particularly influencing context, that of international and regional institutions and their impact on defining relations among languages and peoples. Martín Ruano stresses the asymmetries of the multicultural order and the contradictions present in translation practices that engender or perpetuate inequalities. By critically examining the discourse on legal and institutional translation, Martín Ruano identifies narratives and practices that exercise symbolic violence on linguistic minorities in the international arena. The author warns against the perils that translation and interpreting practices ideologically aligned with centers of power pose to diversity in postmonolingual societies.

Gernot Hebenstreit acknowledges the challenge posed by the use of translation and interpreting as power practices and, in his chapter ("Translating and interpreting cultures. Discussing translation and interpreting ethics in a postmonolingual age"), the author stresses the need to reach an agreement on the ethical stance from which translators and interpreters can better serve diverse societies. Hebenstreit signals the need to work on ethics at a conceptual and theoretical level and reviews Erich Prunč's concept of 'translation culture,' a subsystem of a culture including all agents and resources pertaining to translation and interpreting (Prunč 1997). Like any other culture, translation culture is defined by a set of common values guiding and organizing individual actions. The chapter sets value theory at the center of the discussion on translation culture, and two of the most widely known approaches to translation ethics – Chesterman's (2001) and Prunč's (2005) – are examined. After reviewing the values underpinning both proposals, Hebenstreit encourages the adoption of postmonolingual perspectives on translation and interpreting practices that stress values such as *ecologicality* and *cooperativeness* in pursuing a democratic translation culture.

Michael Cronin ("Translation and Climate Justice: Minority Perspectives") expands the debate by including non-human considerations in the need to manage diversity in order to ensure social justice. In his chapter, Cronin explores the interactions between climate and human beings to stress the importance of taking climate change into account in understanding the dynamics and results of intercultural encounters. As a novel contribution, Cronin's approach stresses the inclusion of non-human collectives in examining human actions, particularly in relation to climate justice, thus enriching the intergroup understanding which lies at the core of translation and interpreting ethics.

De Pedro Ricoy, Andrade Ciudad and Howard are the authors of the first contribution in this volume to describe practical experiences using translation and interpreting policies to manage diversity ("The role of indigenous interpreters in the Peruvian intercultural, bilingual justice system"). This particular chapter focuses on the training of indigenous translators and interpreters in Peru in developing a State-based strategy for providing access to translation and interpreting in the justice system. Situations of conflict between the myriad of cultural traditions sharing the country are used to highlight the problems of a multicultural society with patent power imbalances between different ethnic groups, how translators and interpreters mediate such imbalances and the constraints imposed on and reactions triggered by their practices.

Shuang Li's chapter ("Translation and Interpreting Policies in China: Ethnic Linguistic Minorities in the Judicial System") describes the translation and interpreting policies practiced in China to provide access to justice to national linguistic minorities. Disparities between legislation and practices are highlighted using a complexity approach that considers translation management, translation practices, and translation beliefs as interrelated aspects in determining the possibilities of minoritized communities.

Jiménez Salcedo ("The asymmetry of Canada's language policy regarding access to justice: a model for managing postmonolingualism") describes the evolution of the Canadian court system's stance on translation and interpreting. This chapter suggests that two sets of rights, one for speakers of the country's official languages and one for allophone communities, imply a conception of linguistic rights as second to procedural guarantees and a perception of translation and interpreting as imperfect solutions for adequate access to justice.

The purpose of the book is to afford insights into the interdependence between translation and our postmonolingual condition to inform current discussions on diversity. The different contributors offer varying theoretical perspectives and practical approaches that can shed light on the issues inherent in managing linguistically and culturally complex societies. All of these approaches and experiences converge in the idea that modern societies cannot provide an environment where all their integrating identities have a real possibility to thrive without translation and interpreting. Our diversities are here to stay and their management is our shared responsibility and common endeavor.

References

Beetham, David, 2017. Democracy: universality and diversity. *Ethics & Global Politics*, 2(4), 284-296.

Chesterman, Andrew, 2001. Proposal for a Hieronymic Oath. *The Translator*, 7(2), 139-154.

Cornelius, Wayne A. & Marc R. Rosenblum, 2005. Immigration and Politics. *Annual Review of Political Science*, 8(1), 99-119.

Foucault, Michel, 1975. *Surveiller et punir : naissance de la prison* ['Discipline and Punish: The Birth of the Prison']. Paris: Gallimard.

Gogolin, Ingrid, 1994. *Der monolinguale Habitus der multilingualen Schule* ['The monolingual habitus of the multilingual school']. Münster: Waxmann.

———, 2009. Streitfall Zweisprachigkeit – The Bilingualism Controversy: Les Preludes. *In:* Ingrid Gogolin & Ursula Neumann, eds. *Streitfall Zweisprachigkeit – The Bilingualism Controversy.* Wiesbaden: VS Verlag für Sozialwissenschaften.

Grigoriadis, Ioannis N., 2018. *Democratic Transition and the Rise of Populist Majoritarianism. Constitutional Reform in Greece and Turkey.* Cham: Palgrave Macmillan.

Hammer, Mitchell R., 2015. The Developmental Paradigm for Intercultural Competence Research. *International Journal of Intercultural Relations*, 48, 12-13.

Marzà, Anna & Isabel Ríos, 2016. La reflexió interlingüística a l'educació infantil: una eina per a l'aproximació a la llengua escrita [Interlinguistic reflection in early education: a tool to approach written language]. *Llengua, societat i comunicació: revista de sociolingüística de la Universitat de Barcelona*, 14, 38-46.

Molines Galarza, Núria, 2017. La traducción de la variedad geográfica minorizada: responsabilidad y ética desde la deconstrucción. *In:* Esther Monzó Nebot & Juan Jiménez Salcedo, eds. *Les llengües minoritzades en l'ordre postmonolingüe = Minoritized languages under a postmonolingual order = Las lenguas minorizadas en el orden postmonolingüe.* Castelló de la Plana: Universitat Jaume I, 45-56.

Monzó Nebot, Esther & Juan Jiménez-Salcedo, eds., 2017. *Les llengües minoritzades en l'ordre postmonolingüe,* Castelló de la Plana: Publicacions de la Universitat Jaume I.

OECD (Organization for Economic Cooperation and Development), 2016. *Preparing our Youth for an Inclusive and Sustainable World. The OECD PISA global competence framework,* Paris: OECD.

Prunč, Erich, 1997. Translationskultur (Versuch einer konstruktiven Kritik des translatorischen Handelns) ['Translation and Interpreting Culture (attempting a constructive critique of translational action)']. *TEXTconTEXT,* 11(2), 99-127.

———, 2005. Translationsethik. *In:* Peter Sandrini, ed. *Fluctuat nec mergitur.* Frankfurt am Main: Lang, 165-194.

Rawls, John, 1971. *A Theory of Justice.* Cambridge: Harvard University Press.

Sennett, Richard, 1978. *The Fall of Public Man: On the Social Psychology of Capitalism.* New York: Vintage Books.

Stokes, Bruce, 2017. *What It Takes to Be Truly "One of Us",* Washington: Pew Research Center. Online: http://assets.pewresearch.org/wp-content/uploads/sites/2/2017/02/01092801/Pew-Research-Center-National-Identity-Report-FINAL-February-1-2017.pdf.

UNESCO, 2001. Universal Declaration on Cultural Diversity, 31st Session, Paris, Records of the General Conference.

UNGA (United Nations General Assembly), 2015. Transforming our world: the 2030 Agenda for Sustainable Development Goals, A/RES/70/1, New York, United Nations. Online: https://sustainabledevelopment.un.org/post2015/transformingourworld.

Vertovec, Steven, 2007. Super-diversity and its Implications. *Ethnic and Racial Studies,* 30(6), 1024-1054.

Wason, Peter C., 1960. On the failure to eliminate hypotheses in a conceptual task. *Quarterly Journal of Experimental Psychology,* 12(3), 129-140.

———, 1968. On the failure to eliminate hypotheses... -a second look. *In:* Peter C. Wason & Philip N. Johnson-Laird, eds. *Thinking and reasoning.* Harmondsworth: Penguin, 165-174.

Yildiz, Yasemin, 2012. *Beyond the Mother Tongue: The postmonolingual condition.* New York: Fordham University Press.

Chapter 2

Translators and interpreters as agents of diversity. Managing myths and pursuing justice in postmonolingual societies

Esther Monzó-Nebot

The myth of the Tower of Babel has been used in Western thought to equate diversity with chaos but also to cherish the world's enriching differences. By dealing with multilingualism as a curse that needs handling to prevent chaos or a blessing requiring adequate management policies to harness difference, societies privilege two different approaches to intergroup relations – assimilationism or multiculturalism – and two different views on translators and interpreters, as friends or foes. This chapter addresses how assimilationist and multiculturalist approaches to otherness may impact intergroup relations in globalized societies. To do so, the chapter explores how the idea of translation and interpreting is inextricably tied to societies' conception of otherness; how justice is construed in a dialogic relation to the others; how we organize social spaces in groups of *wedoms* and *theydoms*; how a group's ethical stance and cultural heritage impact its relations with other groups; how cognitive biases and rationalization of injustice enacted upon others may lead a group to act against its own ethical positions in pursuing group- and elite-specific interests; how such pursuit may impact a society's prospects to thrive; and how translation and interpreting may encourage a postmonolingual stance that furthers democracy and resilience in a globalized world. In a context where monolingual and monocultural societies are no longer realistic options due to the speed and volume of demographic flows, this chapter advances a postmonolingual idea of social justice and of the role translators and interpreters play.

The myths in Babel

Translation and interpreting have been represented in cultural imaginaries as building bridges (Dryden 1697 [2014]; Beck 2006), pontiffing (Puig i Ferreter 1975), linking networks (Cronin 2006), matchmaking (see Chengfa 2007, p. 221), midwifering (see Bistué 2013, p. 30-31), or painting and sculpting artworks (Bruni 1424/1426 [2014]; Gotsched 1743, cited in Lefevere 1992, p. 57). These and other metaphors code, enshrine, circulate, and naturalize myths of what translation and interpreting represent in society, thereby conferring differing shares of power to practitioners and establishing a culture-bound definition of what lies within and beyond the limits of translation and interpreting. One of such myths and symbols has been particularly pervasive in Western thought. Benjamin (1923 [1972]), Steiner (1975), Derrida (1985), de Man (1991), or Eco (1991; 1993; 1995) are but a few to explore the significance of the Tower of Babel, a human endeavor of titanic dimensions to build a tower that would allow direct access to the Almighty. The venture was brought to an end when God decided to thwart human's will to power by enforcing multilingualism so that workers could no longer understand each other – or, even worse, so that they would think they did recognize each other's words but would realize only too late that the terms conveyed incompatible meanings:

> Thus one said to his fellow-worker, 'Bring me water' whereupon he would give him earth, at which he struck him and split his skull; 'Bring me an axe' but he brought him a spade, at which he struck him and split his skull. Thus it is written, through their own lips I will destroy them. (Freedman and Simon 1939, p. 309)

The chaos created by forms perceived as familiar which actually carried unfamiliar meanings rendered cooperation chimeric. We humans were craving the knowledge beyond our reach[1] and unbearable suffering ensued: diversity and (the resulting) misunderstanding. The interpretations given to the myth bespeak how uncomfortable human beings feel with adjusting to difference and with the uncertainty of otherness. Diversity is a curse, an unsolvable problem that endlessly frustrates the ambitions of human beings. To prevent further damage, tradition codes the evil nature of difference in a myth, the Tower of Babel, so that our collective memory can warn future generations against any actions that may bring about similar consequences. This fear, instilled through our narrative heritage, serves as a caution against

---

[1] See Ladmiral (2004) on the myriad of relationships between language and knowledge, translation studies and philosophy, Babel and Logos.

ever challenging the *statu quo* again, establishes a model to relate to power centers, and links multilingualism to disempowerment.

The power of that fear, however, may actually derive from, rather than the impossibility of mutual understanding, the inescapable dependence on translators for accomplishing our most titanic enterprises, for any and all issues a culture can no longer solve within the limits of its own heritage. Acknowledging the need of translators and interpreters entails looking at a culture's limits, and the restlessness that drives humans to dispense with translators and interpreters altogether is the anxiety caused by the otherness they cannot comprehend. Under this perspective, Babel is a myth encapsulating the way we relate to the foreign as much as it is about translation. It is a fable on individuality and the imposed silence calls for an acceptance of translation, rather than representing its birth (Steiner 1975, p. 49). From a different but complementary angle, López Guix (2007, p. 3) suggests that the myth, particularly the confusion, would refer to God removing translators from the construction site, imposing a thunderous and painful silence between individuals speaking different languages. Translators were always there and it was them who enabled humans to reach for the skies. To disempower humanity, they had to be impounded.

The thus enforced incapacity for communicating interculturally causes a folly of agony. "Enforced silence is painful" (Berman 2013) and treatment is needed. Assimilationist solutions encourage doing away with any differences to crack the code of the biblical confusion and reenter paradise as one. *E pluribus unum* postulates a nostalgic strife for the fabled primal unity of languages that enables understanding without mediation, a melting pot without difference. Assimilation *handles* multilingualism and ethnicity resorting to the establishment of not only a *lingua franca* but also an *identitas franca*. Under an assimilationist conception of society, identity differences are barriers to social cohesion and sustaining culturally heterogeneous societies reproduces and perpetuates discrimination (Kazal 1995). Early theorists of assimilation and acculturation usually suggested that the distinctive customs of a group would disappear after the immigrants themselves gave way to a second generation (Zangwill 1925), leaving host cultures not only as the majority culture but as the only culture. The resulting absence of differences was hoped to ensure equal opportunities for all. Later studies, however, showed how the children of immigrants are culturally assimilated but remain a *social* distinctive group (Glazer and Moynihan 1963). Doing away with one's heritage does not ensure perfect social mobility and, indeed, sociocultural differences tend to be accentuated when a threat to a group's distinctive features and integrity is felt, even if it is the dominant culture that is challenged (Verkuyten 2009). Later revisions of the approach acknowledge diversity as an irreducible condition but advocate for a colorblindness that can focus on the shared traits of diverse populations. Colorblindness demands minimizing the attention given to cultural differences suggesting that an accentuation of idiosyncratic features and otherness may lead to negative stereotypes (Anthony 2012). The underlying assumption is that we, as humans, react negatively to difference.

This view has been abandoned in the international arena. Governments all over the world enshrined the immanent value of cultural diversity by signing the Convention on the Protection and Promotion of the Diversity of Cultural Expressions (UNESCO General Conference 2005), which acknowledges the essential role of cultural diversity in maintaining peace within and between nations. Further, empirical studies have helped us realize that people who see greater differences between ethnic groups, rather than focus on their shared traits, also see their value and consider those groups more positively while feeling more secure in their own identity (Wolsko et al. 2006). Indeed, *in varietate concordia* can be said to represent multiculturalists embracing a globalized landscape of blurring boundaries by showing a determination to understand otherness and *managing* the paths towards effective communication (see a comment of Llull's work in Eco 1991) across the different territories of the globe but also within national frontiers. The basic assumption is that diversity will not evolve into sameness, not even with institutional intervention, and that achieving a prosperous society requires a (mediated) dialogue between differences. Contrary to what assimilationism sustains, multiculturalists hold that "affirmation toward one's ethnic group leads to a positive ethnic identity and higher levels of acceptance toward ethnic outgroups" (Verkuyten 2005; 2010), thereby favoring social harmony and intergroup cooperation.

Both approaches seek the best way out of an apparent chaos to land a perfect and harmonious society. The underlying question may be posed as follows: does a democratic society function most effectively when we enforce our unity or when we cherish our diversity? Research conducted within the field of Translation and Interpreting Studies embraces its share of responsibility in the solution of the puzzle of social cohesion and global cooperation by revisiting the myths on which Babel is grounded: Are translators and interpreters a sign of our failure or "le signe de réconciliations entre tous ces hommes qui se tuent encore parce qu'ils parlent des langues différentes"[2] (Eco 1993, p. 206)?

---

[2] "The sign of reconciliation between all those men who still kill each other because they speak different languages" (author's translation).

A postmonolingual idea of justice

Modern societies have been accommodating diversity in different manners for some decades (Vertovec 2010) and policymakers now face an enhanced diversity that continues to grow and can only be expected to maintain its upward trend (Cornelius and Rosenblum 2005). In democratic systems, committed to equal representation (Beetham 2017), negotiation among the different interests is the key to finding the arrangement that works best for all. Reactions to diversity have been dissimilar and both individual members and policy-making bodies have not always approached negotiations with other identities "without holding their strangeness against them" (Bauman 2000, p. 104). From differing perspectives, the idea that the constitutive will to cooperate is the keystone of societies (Rawls 1971, p. 4, 29) is basic to elaborations on justice and social justice.

To ensure a society's wellbeing and progress, cooperation among all its different members must be pursued. This requires a system that can satisfy the interests of the individuals and garner their wills. The finesse required from such an endeavor against the increasing diversity becomes more evident when considering that slightly different configurations of the rules governing the system may result in increased benefits for specific groups of people and decreased advantages for others. In tipping the balance towards one of the available options, the unforced force of the better argument (Habermas 1992, p. 133) is the weapon to determine the solutions to be implemented, but negotiation can only be truthful to the democratic principle of political representation when diversity is recognized (see Lash and Featherstone 2002, and Martín Ruano, this volume), when all communities are allowed to voice their own positions on equal footing. This entails demanding morally unjustified inequalities to be corrected (Rawls 1971, p. 16), including those caused by one's class, gender, native language or culture. Those baseline inequalities are, according to Rawls, the very matter of justice (Rawls 1971, p. 38), and the role of democratic institutions (Rawls 1971, p. 6) is, rather than providing a level playing field (i.e. the same rules for everyone), to consider how the structure of society impacts individuals' opportunities and to distribute justice accordingly, always subject to the inviolability of civil and political rights (Rawls 1971, p. 474 ff). Rawls perspective has been subject to criticism for its unawareness of the cultural and linguistic differences inherent in the ideas that underpin his views on justice (Peled and Bonotti 2016). Social justice in a diverse environment requires institutions to proactively understand the diverging and sometimes conflicting positions from which their citizens can voice their differences, be heard and taken into account.

Democratic societies have implemented specific policies to prevent discrimination, restore the damages caused by discriminatory and biased practices, and correct inequalities (see Fishman 1986; Singh 1995; Strachan et al. 2004; Gomes de Andrade 2005; Toggenburg 2005; He et al. 2007). To truly ensure equality without expunging diversity, privilege must be acknowledged (Johnson 2006), the fallacies of decontextualizing individual efforts from their sociocultural backgrounds must be exposed (Sen 1980), and the interest of what others have to say must be genuinely valued (Gadamer 1960, p. 363-364) as a contribution to our own capacity to understand the world and its issues.

Revisiting the Tower of Babel, Oakeshott (1962) sees the impiety of reaching to heaven as an inclination to follow one's moral system unaware of any other. When faced with such enterprises, it is the role of society to treasure variety and protect justice by leveling the field and ending unilateral endeavors. Oakeshott condemns, as so did the Almighty in the original fable, the excessive pursuit of any value at the expense of others, especially the imposition of institutional solutions that are blind to otherness and incongruent with communities' history and traditions (1962, p. 65).

The problems deriving from the diversity blindness against which Oakeshott cautioned have been reported in recent efforts for global organization and peace building (Park 2010). Even when having peace at heart, peace-building forces impose one particular conceptualization of the justice and the rule of law upon local legal practices and institutions, evincing the contradictions of the project of assimilation: while claiming cultural neutrality, the culture of sameness is enforced and local cultures are domesticated, at best, to conform to a depoliticized multiculturalism. As commendable and desirable as it is, the "human family" (UNGA 1948) as an end can be approached using more or less assimilationist and more or less multicultural courses of action.

Rather than compelling others to embrace a particular conception of social organization and justice, Sen's approach focuses on an institutional intervention limited to the correction of injustices (2009). The impact of injustice on a person's wellbeing is the point of departure for Sen's discussion of his idea of justice and also the topic of his first quote (2009, p. vii):

> "In the little world in which children have their existence whosoever brings them up, there is nothing so finely perceived and so finely felt, as injustice" (Dickens [1861] 2011, p. 60)

Such distress is equally valid for adults and a strong moving force. It was the need to stop injustice, rather than the search for a perfectly just world, that moved Parisians to storm the Bastille and that gave force to the civil rights movement in the United States (2009, p. vii). For Sen, being moved by other's pain and humiliation ensures that we can approach situations and comparatively assess the choices that advance justice and reduce injustice (2009, p. 414-415). Understanding, sympathizing and arguing are basic human abilities that allow us to communicate, also interculturally, and communication is the only path that can enable cooperation, allowing us to escape silence and isolation (2009, p. 415). Under Sen's perspective, competing rights, which can be expected from competing interests and ideas of good in a diverse society, can be settled by dialogically and comparatively assessing freedoms, always considering the real contexts and individuals' actual *capabilities* to lead their lives. In his discussion of justice, Sen makes a point in distinguishing *opportunity* from *choice* (2009, p. 229). When a person has the option to stay at home or go out, they have freedom of choice. If that person is under house arrest, the same opportunities are available, but consequences differ and so the choice is constricted. Duress, which may be applied through physical force or may be the consequence of actual access to material or intellectual resources, must be factored in when establishing the resulting freedoms in every situation.

In adopting this process-oriented stance, Sen discourages a focus on *niti*-centered principles and safeguarding institutions and claims that attention should be directed to the practical problems of a *nyaya*-based just society (2009, p. 67):

> Consider two different words – *niti* and *nyaya* – both of which stand for justice in classical Sanskrit. Among the principal uses of the term *niti* are organizational propriety and behavioural correctness. In contrast with *niti*, the term *nyaya* stands for a comprehensive concept of realized justice. In that line of vision, the roles of institutions, rules and organiz- ation, important as they are, have to be assessed in the broader and more inclusive perspective of *nyaya*, which is inescapably linked with the world that actually emerges, not just the institutions or rules we happen to have. (Sen 2009, p. 20)

The communicative approach in establishing a permanent dialogue with otherness is also present in Scanlon's discussion of competing rights in multiethnic and multicultural societies (Scanlon 2003). In a seemingly contradictory fashion, Scanlon defines rights as constraints on the discretion of individuals or institutions to act (2003, p. 3). The key to such limitations is that restrictions would only be imposed when they constitute necessary and feasible means to prevent unacceptable results, particularly attempts "to restrict individuals' personal lives as a way of controlling the evolution of mores" (Scanlon 2003, p. 192). To determine the existence of such restrictions, all groups and perspectives within societies must be able to voice their positions. The key idea in Scanlon's approach is that we must consider others as equal members of society and equally entitled to play a role in determining how society evolves (2003, p. 190), also in the "informal politics of social life" (ibid.).

The aforementioned views on justice share an interest in understanding otherness through dialogue between culturally and socially diverse communities – a dialogue that can hardly be fathomed without translators and interpreters. Without mediation, social justice becomes as chimeric as the ambition to reach heaven. Can we realistically expect culture-bound beings to assess dominant institutions as the product of a specific tradition? Can we trust them to realize the competing values underlying each other's idea of good and justice? In what follows I will discuss the processes underlying intergroup relations that can endanger intergroup cooperation in order to determine how translators and interpreters are instrumental in an idea of justice that can fit the demands of Babel.

The formation of social groups and the creation of otherness

Humans need interpersonal relationships on evolutionary grounds (Baumeister and Leary 1995). It is through social relationships that we can ensure survival, fulfill our needs and achieve happiness (Haller and Hadler 2006). In our relations, humans create ties based on different features such as ethnic origin, age, gender or language. Such relations build the basis for emotional attachment to a specific social group and allow us to develop a social identity, which is key to our wellbeing, particularly to our self-esteem (Tajfel and Turner 1979). In building the ingroup, that is, the group of socially bound humans sharing a core set of characteristics with us, the ties linking its members also distinguish and create divisions from those who do not share the same features. The result is the organization of any social space in diverse *wedoms* and *theydoms*.

Barth's social interaction model (1969) actually suggests that it is a distinction from others which allows a group to develop its social identity. This would mean that the features defining a group's identity will vary according to the identities with which they share any given socio-cultural system (Barth 1969, p. 14). According to his model, (ethnic) groups organize themselves around two sets of distinctions: signs, which are overt, and may include features such as language or clothing, and values, which provide guidelines for behavior and moral judgment (Barth 1969, p. 14). Sharing moral values has a binding (and blinding) power and the fact that social groupings are tied by a common moral basis (Haidt 2007; 2012) implies the coexistence of (slightly) different moral orders within the same social space. Given that human thinking is based on socially-learned moral and emotional reactions

(Haidt 2001; 2012), the values of a particular group play an important role in processing the information and constructing social experiences, allowing for different information and experiences to be perceived by different social groups.

The idea that our values and emotions filter everything we perceive from the empirical world is far from new (Bruner and Postman 1947; Veltkamp et al. 2008). Also, Translation and Interpreting Studies acknowledges the impact of values, especially the dominant values of institutions engaging translators and interpreters, in both practice (Venuti 1998) and academic reflection (Tymoczko 2007). The following section will discuss contributions on how values impact our relations to otherness.

Evaluating values

In his seminal work on prejudice, Allport (1954) suggested that humans have an 'evaluative bias' which makes them assess the value of their own social group by permanent comparison to other social groups. Also from a social psychology approach, Zajonc (1980) suggested that human minds automatically evaluate everything they perceive. Several models have been developed within the field of cognitive psychology to shed light on how humans process information. Chen and Chaiken (1999) developed a model which supports Zajonc's idea. In their model, information is processed following a dual system. The first system, a symbol-based heuristic system, is the default method that we apply in understanding our experiences by associating any new events with past episodes and the lessons we learned from the successful or unsuccessful outcomes of our behavior. In order to process information in such a way, we have no need to consciously activate any thinking on the matter and responses may be triggered immediately. However, a conscious effort is needed for the systematic processing to take over. Even when this second system is activated, biases may lead individuals to make up reasons to perceive what they wanted to perceive and act on their perceptions as they wanted to act in the first place (Wilson 2002). Similar models have been developed adding details as to the interaction of memory and rules (Smith and DeCoster 2000), the coordination or dissociation of both systems under particular circumstances (Nosek 2007), and the impact of each one on behavior (Strack and Deutsch 2004). They all seem to agree on the default processing being heuristic, that is, a gut reaction based on pre-formed ideas and rules learned in the sociocultural context. The systematic processing would only be activated under special circumstances.

In intergroup relations, the emotional attachment to other members of our ingroups derives in an ingroup *affinity*, a positive evaluation of the group representing our social identity and a need to protect its position within society (see Sporer 2001). This translates in an inclination towards those with whom we share an identity and a tendency to evaluate them more positively than any outgrouper. Empirical studies have provided evidence that, when asked to allocate limited or unlimited resources to groups under different circumstances (distribute budgets, awards, etc.), individuals show a strong tendency to benefit ingroupers, but also to discriminate against outgroupers even when no direct benefit can be expected for the members of the ingroup (Tajfel and Billic 1974; Mucchi-Faina et al. 2002; Rubini et al. 2016). As we strive to achieve or maintain a positive social identity, the position and distinctiveness of our group becomes a valuable we need to protect. We need our group to be *good*, but we also need it to be *better*. When a threat to that goodness is perceived, an instinctive protection triggers the activation of intergroup biases, increased affinity towards co-members of the ingroup and hostility towards the outgroup, perceived as a threat. Thus, the outgroup becomes a target of negative emotions, dislike, derogation, and hostility. The categorical bias, that is, the tendency to classify what is perceived under known categories, will contribute to such hostility by preventing individualized knowledge of the subject once their otherness – and, in a situation of threat, also antagonistic position – has been assessed. Attributes previously assigned to the outgroup as a whole will be blindly applied to the new subject. The categorical bias was thought to be inherent to human nature for decades (Allport 1954). However, studies (Bargh 1994; Spencer et al. 1998) have attested to the motivational basis of assigning subjects to categories with preconceived attributes instead of processing their individual characteristics. More specifically, empirical studies have suggested a motivational link between the individual's self-perception and the organization of their social space in categories of human beings. These categories are activated when perceivers can position themselves in a higher social or moral stance by assigning others to groups whose attributes can be looked down to. This suggests that individuals enduring hardships and lowered self-esteem may become more prone to categorical thinking and prejudice (Plous 2003).

Indeed, the Downward Comparison Theory suggests that, when experiencing negative affect (for instance, when feeling discriminated against), individuals comparing themselves to lower-status groups will enhance their sense of wellbeing (Wills 1981; 1990). This seems to imply that individuals will derogate lower-status groups even when their negative feelings are the result of derogation or threat from higher-status groups. Such a conundrum takes renewed interest in a moment where the growing lethality of intergroup conflict is threatening to cause the collapse of global social organization (Wright 2009), but also in a moment where global demographic changes make the liquidity of modern times (Bauman 2000) more relevant than ever and where global standardization threatens diversity in general and underprivileged groups and minorities in particular.

On a more encouraging note, the contact hypothesis (Williams 1947; Allport 1954) suggests that frequency of contact may lead to the debunking of the intergroup biases that generate and escalate conflicts between different groups. Increased liking and positive affect (Bornstein 1989), decategorization of individuals and reduction of stereotypical thinking (Schneider 2003) have all been linked to sustained contact between members of different groups. The effects of contact occur irrespective of any physical occurrence, as contact mediated via narratives, especially narratives voiced by members of the same ingroup, maintains its effects ('extended contact hypothesis,' see Wright et al. 1997). The role translators and interpreters play in the circulation of otherness (Heilbron and Sapiro 2002; Hung 2005) and the potential of proactive translation and interpreting policies in deactivating intergroup conflict cannot be overstated.

The political use of intergroup relations

The organization of societies in emotionally-laden wedoms and theydoms, together with the prevalence of sociocultural rules in human reasoning are two particularly convenient factors for what has been termed "symbolic politics" (Edelman 1971). Symbolic politics states that most of our claims and perceptions are based on symbols and myths conveyed by the narratives constructing the identity of a group (Kaufman 2001). This theory does not question the truth behind those symbols and myths and converges in the general idea that narratives are a means towards rationalizing worldviews and purposes (Wilson 2002). As Edelman states, human beings have the capacity to reconstruct the past, perceive the present, and anticipate the future using symbols that "abstract, screen, condense, distort, displace, and even create" the input received from the senses (Edelman 1971, p. 2). Symbols encapsulate a network of narratives that resonate with our moral beliefs and have, therefore, the capacity to arouse ideas and actions. Invoking a symbol can evoke emotions of anger, despise, grievance, pride or attachment because they encode sociocultural meanings (Schöpflin 1997) that lie at the basis of our heuristic thinking. Such shorthand references are used in rituals and myths which are shared and recognized by the members of a group and tied to other symbols in a network of narratives that explains and provides meaning to a particular social identity. Armstrong called this network the "myth-symbol complex" and stressed its role in boundary work (1982), not only because ingroupers act by those symbols but also because those symbols and myths are used to define identities, to extol and glorify heroes and to demean enemies. Narratives make sense of the values of right and wrong and tie them to ingroupers' and outgroupers' identities.

Being key in rational thinking, the ability to process symbols has had a fundamental role in the evolution of human beings, especially in their efforts to organize themselves collectively and form what the United Nations termed the "human family" (UNGA 1948). The counterpart is that inflexible attachments to illusions and misperceptions are made possible on the very same basis, blocking receptivity to incompatible information (Edelman 1971, p. 44). Confirmation bias is the tendency to seek evidence that corroborates what we already think and to disregard anything that challenges our beliefs (Beattie and Baron 1988). Evidence supporting the myths building our identity will be immediately processed by the default heuristic system without any need to activate the systematic processing. Any evidence against the myths, which may endanger the myth-symbol complex and therefore the group's social identity, will face the confirmation bias and our capacity to use the systematic processing to rationalize any new evidence and make it fit the narrative constructing our social identity. On the contrary, any narratives purporting to strengthen the identity of the group, reinforcing myths and using the symbols that resonate with ingroupers will be comfortably and quickly processed. Symbolic politics focuses on how myths and biases can be exploited to advance specific agendas by garnering the public's support.

The rise of narratives intimating hostility and hatred towards one or several social identities, offering simplified representations of the world, a known order in the middle of changing socioeconomic conditions, conferring meaning to our existence beyond any present circumstances has been feeding intergroup hostility across the globe. Particularly, the rise of intolerant speech against migrants seeking international protection has been abundantly echoed in the media, triggering action in the face of well-founded concerns that it may fuel terror attacks (Bender 2016; Faiola 2016). On May 31, 2016, the European Commission issued a voluntary Code of Conduct on Countering Illegal Hate Speech Online that requires major Internet companies to remove all instances of hate speech from their sites (Fioretti and Chee 2016). One year later, on May 10, 2017, the Digital Single Market Strategy confirmed the need to continue those efforts (European Commission 2017) and other initiatives (Angwin et al. 2017) are also pointing at the flaws of big social media to effectively protect their users against hate. Step by step, "invisible crimes" (Jupp et al. 1999) against diversity are coming in focus of the criminological telescope.

Recent populist discourses targeted against minorities, especially migrants, are undermining the world's idea of justice, socially, politically and cognitively (Stychin 2004; Zick et al. 2011; Winter and Teitelbaum 2013;

Zbarauskaitė et al. 2015) by depicting diversity as a threat to the superiority of ingroups and triggering protective reactions that impede the understanding of strangers and their otherness and preclude the negotiations necessary to achieve social justice, both in formal and informal day-to-day politics. The results on targeted groups are devastating, as overt and covert discrimination and hate demoralize, demotivate and demobilize individuals (Hinduja and Patchin 2007; Henson et al. 2013), endangering the constitutive cooperation within societies. When voiced by the elites, intergroup hatred appeals those who have aspirations to access a higher status group (Postmes and Smith 2009), who tailor their actions to please the members of their coveted ingroup-to-be. Groups bringing hostility to extremes claim the demotion or exclusion of minorities' rights and demands from the political arena. The rights of outgroupers are questioned and denied with varying degrees of rationalization or violence. The acquiescence of the higher-status groups reinforces the perception of discrimination and violence being within the moral limits of the ingroup, even when they are opposed by other parts of society. The effects of explicit endorsement are obviously more damaging to the efforts towards achieving global cooperation and endanger the success of human beings from an evolutionary approach.

To explain such support, the manipulative elite hypothesis has been suggested in analyzing the occurrence of several ethnic wars and genocides, such as those occurred in Europe in the dissolution of the former Republic of Yugoslavia (Denitch 1994, p. 62), the Kurdish conflict in Turkey (Eriten and Romine 1994) or the Rwanda genocide (see Thompson 2007). Kaufman (2001) notices that manipulation cannot work unless a history of conflict is embedded in shared myths and symbols (Edelman 1971). This would provide a basis for symbolic politics to engender intergroup hatred and foster an accord of minds as to the convenience of intergroup violence. The elite-predation model sustains that it is the elite holding power within a group that has an interest in predating other groups and manipulates ingroupers to spur conflict on any fabricated basis which appears rational to those under their influence (protect ethnic myths overseas may be rationalized by a group even if the elite's interest is to allocate public resources to defense industries).

The features defining an identity and bringing ingroupers together, triggering intergroup differentiation and establishing boundaries within a social system and between social systems are flexible (Barth 1969, p. 14; Van den Berghe 1981; Veenstra and Haslam 2000). However, perceptions and available categories to identify oneself and others are educated in socialization processes, biases are forged and reinforced in symbolic interactions, and allegiances, carved in the moral programming, are organized and may be mobilized to ensure a particular, even oppressive, *statu quo* or to fuel conflicts and wars. Such semiotically loaded symbolic interactions are precisely a terrain translators and interpreters walk every day.

Translators and interpreters as diversity experts

Interpreters and translators, such as La Malinche (see Valdeón 2013), are seen as impacting intergroup relations and groups' integrity, sometimes sharing membership to at least one of those groups and also identity features with those for whom they mediate, language at the very least. Apart from their privileged access to knowledge and their necessary intervention for others' to reach heaven, their straddling different social identities may explain the suspicions translators and interpreters have traditionally risen in mediating intergroup relations. The question is whether the opportunities afforded by their bestriding the groups they connect, by their privileged position in understanding and managing post-Babelic chaos can be adequately harnessed in the development of modern societies and the evolution of intergroup relations. Intergroup antagonism enshrined and perpetuated in intergroup myths blocks real dialogue and has already shown its lethal potential. In the century we just left behind and which became known as the "century of genocide" (Levene 2000), conflict based on religion and ethnical origin tore the world apart. This chapter has argued that, in ensuring social justice for all members, based on the recognition of their equal right to decide on the future of our common existence, the anxieties and mistrust triggered by otherness need to give way to a process of mutual understanding. No justice can be achieved without communication between the manifold differences of the myriad of diversities inhabiting the globe. And no communication can be achieved at a global scale without translators and interpreters.

Diversity is indeed a linguistic and cultural issue. When we acknowledge that translators and interpreters are not only linguistic but also cultural mediators – when not experts[3] – we are embracing the complexities of communication and difference. However, diversity is also and mainly a psychosocial matter. Translation and interpreting scholars have been claiming enhanced epistemological domains for both academics and practitioners in order to provide increasingly accurate accounts of the issues impacting translation and interpreting. In recent years, globalization has

---

[3] Although some authors strongly support this cultural expertise as part of task of translators and interpreters (Wolf 1999; Prunč 2004), others challenge the assumption of associated functions, such as providing cultural information that is not present in the original discourse. See Niska (1995) and Bahadır (2004) for contrasting views on the role of interpreters as cultural experts.

exponentially increased the opportunities for cross-cultural, cross-sectional, and cross-disciplinary fertilization to improve the frameworks used to explain the priorities and constraints translators and interpreters must balance and the tools they have at their disposal in pursuing their goals. This global scholarly communication has provided opportunities for contrasting local norms and qualifying general approaches while at the same time disseminating knowledge on settings with limited access, such as asylum-seeking processes (Inghilleri 2003; Pöllabauer 2004; 2008; MacFarlane et al. 2009; Merlini 2009) or war zones (Palmer 2007; Baker 2010; Inghilleri 2010; Inghilleri and Harding 2010; Stahuljak 2010).

The broadened interest for diverse phenomena and enhanced theoretical and methodological approaches is paving the way for studying known and new factors from a variety of perspectives with the potential of changing how we explain translation and interpreting but also what we require from translators and interpreters and what we tell society they can expect from translation and interpreting. This is the case of an increasing number of studies on the ethics of translators and interpreters (Björn 2005; Tymoczko 2006; Chesterman 2009; Baker and Maier 2011; Floros 2012; Drugan and Tipton 2017) and on the psychosocial factors impacting their contexts (Angelelli 2004; Elghezouani 2007; Leanza 2007), their performance (Berthold and Fischman 2014), and wellbeing (Lipton et al. 2002).

The psychosocial factors in intergroup relations impact translators' and interpreters' work and may frustrate their attempts at opening up "the space of mediation" (Cronin 2006, p. 135) between different sociocultural groups and identities, which transcend cultural differences, by resisting cultural mediation. Managing the biases discussed in this contribution (e.g. Edelman 1971, p. 44; Tajfel and Billic 1974; Mucchi-Faina et al. 2002; Rubini et al. 2016), by which any information not conforming to identity expectations may be disregarded and obliterated, falls within the scope of what has been termed *diversity intelligence* (Hughes 2014, p. 67), "the ability to navigate broad social, cultural, racial, and other human diversities and to comprehend and appropriately use extensive knowledge of diversity" (Hughes 2016, p. 5). Interpreters and translators need not only to be aware of intergroup antagonistic myth-symbol networks and resulting socialized prejudices and biases but also to appropriately act on such representations to allow for a real understanding in communicative situations.

Identities are owned by the person (Heider 1958), which means that they become a part of themselves but also that they are at the disposal of individuals to strategically negotiate their social interactions (cf Weigert et al. 1986, p. 23). Symbolic encounters where language and cultural differences encumber understanding are the share of the process of justice that we can entrust to translation and interpreting. By encouraging a "reflexive project of self" (e.g. Giddens 1977, p. 32-33), we bring translators and interpreters closer to mastering otherness, for their own and others' sake.

Eco wondered whether thinking of translation and interpreting as the non-dogmatic and non-repressive way to achieve understanding and peace was a rhetorical enterprise (Eco 1993, p. 207), and translation and interpreting scholars have long been voicing claims that increased attention should be paid to "issues such as class, gender, race" (Cronin 2002, p. 46). Knowledge on how such issues impact any mediated communication needs to be developed and transferred so that translators and interpreters can challenge role assumptions and develop strategies within the boundaries of their expertise to live up to the challenge of effectively overcoming cultural boundaries and engaging citizens in cross-identity dialogue. Their strategies can determine how the perils and displays of intergroup conflict evolve and how society faces post-Babelic anxieties and provides a secure environment for continuous social and economic growth (Dharmapala and McAdams 2005; Parekh 2005; Harvey 2012; Mason 2013; Chakraborti 2015). With the help of translators and interpreters, Babel may become "come torre ferma, che non crolla già mai la cima per soffiar di venti"[4] (Alighieri [1304-1321] 1985, p. 48-49).

Conclusion

This chapter has focused on how our present and future societies need the development and finer tuning of multiculturalist policies which include translation and interpreting as a tool to enable and empower our increasingly diverse societies. The drawbacks for prosperity and peace efforts of individual and institutional blindness to differences, needs and interests among identities have been highlighted. The role of institutions in designing the best arrangement for justice has been said to be impracticable against current social realities without proactive translation and interpreting policies. The process of aligning the basic structure of societies for all their members requires acknowledging the rights of all concerned to decide on our collective futures, to speak and be heard, to be offered an escape from the painful Babelic silence and be granted a voice in the negotiations of social contracts. As the Catalan author Mercè Rodoreda stresses, "voler ofegar la paraula és voler aturar la vida" (Rodoreda 1974, p. 13), attempting to stifle the word is an attempt to impede life. Society needs to move forward to face its new challenges.

---

[4] "as a tower firmly set, shakes not its top for any blast that blows" (Alighieri [1304-1321] 2009, p. 164)

Importantly, intergroup communication entails the communication of different value systems, which need to be balanced in configuring the best arrangement for all society members to thrive. Different mechanisms to preclude one view to be erected at the expense of the others, as Oakeshott warned, are available and this chapter has reviewed some of them – Rawls' priority of liberties, Scanton's prevention of unacceptable results, and Sen's correction of injustices. Only constant dialogue and negotiation of societal configurations can realize justice. Only real understanding of diversity can achieve social justice, an endeavor which can only be guaranteed with proactive translation and interpreting policies.

Translation and interpreting are indeed a matter of concern for institutions in democratic societies representing a myriad of identities. The burden of convergence cannot be placed on the shoulders of linguistic and cultural minorities (Peled and Bonotti 2016, p. 809). Through deep understanding and active management of symbols and information processing strategies, translators and interpreters can become the most needed non-dogmatic and non-repressive means to prevent intergroup threats and biases and intimate knowledge on diversity through constant interaction with societies, thus promoting a multiculturalist approach in each and every one of us. A continued translation and interpreting activity within and across our social spaces can help individuals and policy-making bodies navigate diversity. It can also protect us against the sadly thriving populist majoritarianism (Grigoriadis 2018) predating on social identities and diversity and encumbering the very possibility of social justice within democratic societies.

> The war against superstition and the totalitarian mentality is an endless war. In protean forms, it is fought and refought in every country and every generation. [...] Temporary victories can be registered against this, but not permanent ones. [...] But it is in this struggle that we develop the muscles and sinews that enable us to defend civilization, and the moral courage to name it as something worth fighting for. (Hitchens 2011, p. 11)

Throughout the chapter, a focus on process as regards understanding, diversity and justice has been stressed. The liquidity of our present times demands that we acknowledge that the success of diversity management depends on the processes of diversity rather than its contents. Indeed the future accomplishments of our societies rely on sustainable solutions to the tensions between the will to stability and a drive for change (Bauman 2000). For translation and interpreting to impact our future, their presence must be sustained.

References

Alighieri, Dante, [1304-1321] 1985. Purgatorio. Canto quinto. *La Divina Commedia*. Scandicci: La Nuova Italia.

——, [1304-1321] 2009. Purgatory. *The Divine Commedy*, translated by Charles W. Eliot. New York: Cosimo.

Allport, Gordon, 1954. *The Nature of Prejudice*. Reading: Addison Wesley.

Angelelli, Claudia, 2004. *Medical Interpreting and Cross-cultural Communication*. Cambridge, New York: Cambridge University Press.

Angwin, Julia, Ariana Tobin & Madeleine Varner, 2017. *Have You Experienced Hate Speech on Facebook? We Want To Hear From You*, New York: ProPublica. Online: https://www.propublica.org/article/have-you-experienced-hate-speech-on-facebook-we-want-to-hear-from-you.

Anthony, Robert M., 2012. A Challenge to Critical Understandings of Race. *Journal for the Theory of Social Behaviour*, 42(3), 260-282.

Armstrong, John Alexander, 1982. *Nations before Nations*. Chapel Hill: The University of North Carolina Press.

Bahadır, Sebnem, 2004. Moving In-Between: The Interpreter as Ethnographer and the Interpreting-Researcher as Anthropologist. *Meta*, 49(4), 805-821.

Baker, Mona, 2010. Interpreters and translators in the war zone. *The Translator*, 16, 165-173.

Baker, Mona & Carol Maier, 2011. Ethics in Interpreter & Translator Training. *Special Issue of The Interpreter and Translator Trainer*, 5, 1-14.

Bargh, John A., 1994. The Four Horsemen of Automaticity: Awareness, intention, efficiency, and control in social cognition. *In:* Robert S Wyer & Thomas K Srull, eds. *Handbook of Social Cognition*. 2 ed. Hillsdale: Erlbaum, 1-40.

Barth, Fredrik, 1969. Introduction. *Ethnic Groups and Boundaries. The Social Organization of Culture Difference*. Boston: Little, Brown and Company, 9-38.

Bauman, Zygmunt, 2000. *Liquid Modernity*. Cambridge: Polity.

Baumeister, Roy F. & Mark R. Leary, 1995. The Need to Belong: Desire for Interpersonal Attachments as a Fundamental Human Motivation. *Psychological Bulletin*, 117(3), 497-529.

Beattie, Jane & Jonathan Baron, 1988. Confirmation and matching biases in hypothesis testing. *The Quarterly Journal of Experimental Psychology A: Human Experimental Psychology*, 40(A), 269-297.

Beck, Ulrich, 2006. *Cosmopolitan Vision*, translated by Ciaran Cronin. Cambridge: Polity Press.

Beetham, David, 2017. Democracy: universality and diversity. *Ethics & Global Politics*, 2(4), 284-296.

Bender, Ruth, 2016. German Police Carry Out Nationwide Crackdown on Internet Hate Speech, *Wall Street Journal*. Online: http://www.wsj.com/articles/german-police-carry-out-nationwide-crackdown-on-internet-hate-speech-1468429275.

Benjamin, Walter, 1923 [1972]. Die Aufgabe des Übersetzers. *In:* Rolf Tiedemann & Hermann Schweppenhäuser, eds. *Gesammelte Schriften.* Frankfurt am Main: Suhrkamp, 9-21.

Berman, Harold J., 2013. *Law and language. Effective Symbols of Community.* Cambridge: Cambridge University Press.

Berthold, S. Megan & Yael Fischman, 2014. Social Work with Trauma Survivors: Collaboration with Interpreters. *Social Work,* 59(2), 103-110.

Bistué, Belén, 2013. *Collaborative Translation and Multi-Version Texts in Early Modern Europe.* Farnham: Ashgate.

Björn, Gunilla Jarkman, 2005. Ethics and interpreting in psychotherapy with refugee children and families. *Nordic Journal of Psychiatry,* 59, 516-521.

Bornstein, Robert F., 1989. Exposure and affect: Overview and meta-analysis of research, 1968-1987. *Psychological Bulletin,* 106(2), 265-289.

Bruner, Jerome & Leo Postman, 1947. Emotional Selectivity in Perception and Reaction. *Journal of Personality,* 16(1), 69-77.

Bruni, Leonardo, 1424/1426 [2014]. On the correct way to translate (De interpretatione recta). *In:* Douglas Robinson, ed. *Western Translation Theory from Herodotus to Nietzsche.* 2 ed. London: Routledge, 57-60.

Chakraborti, Neil, 2015. Re-thinking hate crime: fresh challenges for policy and practice. *Journal of Interpersonal Violence,* 30(10), 1738-54. Online: http://www.ncbi.nlm.nih.gov/pubmed/25192703.

Chen, Serena & Shelly Chaiken, 1999. The heuristic-systematic model in its broader context. *In:* Shelly Chaiken & Yaacov Trope, eds. *Dual-process theories in social psychology.* New York: Guilford, 73-96.

Chengfa, Yu, 2007. On Qian Zhongshu's 'Theory of Sublimity'. *Perspectives: Studies in Translatology,* 14(3), 214-229.

Chesterman, Andrew, 2009. Ethics of translation. *In:* Mona Baker, ed. *Translation Studies. Critical Concepts in Linguistics.* London, New York: Routledge, 34-43.

Cornelius, Wayne A. & Marc R. Rosenblum, 2005. Immigration and Politics. *Annual Review of Political Science,* 8(1), 99-119.

Cronin, Michael, 2002. The Empire Talks Back: Orality, heteronomy, and the cultural turn in interpretation studies. *In:* Maria Tymoczko & Edwin Gentzler, eds. *Translation and power.* Amherst, Boston: University of Massachusetts Press, 45 62.

———, 2006. *Translation and Identity.* London: Routledge.

Van den Berghe, Pierre, 1981. *The Ethnic Phenomenon.* New York: Elsevier.

Denitch, Bogdan, 1994. *Ethnic Nationalism: The Tragic Death of Yugoslavia.* Minneapolis: University of Minnesota Press.

Derrida, Jacques, 1985. Des tours de Babel. *In:* Joseph F Graham, ed. *Difference in Translation.* London: Cornell University Press, 165-207.

Dharmapala, Dhammika & Richard H. McAdams, 2005. Words That Kill? An Economic Model of the Influence of Speech on Behavior (with Particular Reference to Hate Speech). *The Journal of Legal Studies,* 34(1), 93-136.

Dickens, Charles, [1861] 2011. *Great Expectations.* New York: Barns & Noble.

Drugan, Joanna & Rebecca Tipton, 2017. Translation, ethics and social responsibility. *The Translator*, 23(2), 119-125.

Dryden, John, 1697 [2014]. Steering betwixt two extremes. *In:* Douglas Robinson, ed. *Western Translation Theory from Herodotus to Nietzsche*. London: Routledge, 174-175.

Eco, Umberto, 1991. La lingua universale di Ramon Llull. *Cahiers Ferdinand de Saussure*, 45, 121-149.

———, 1993. Traduction et langue parfaite, in *Assises de la Traduction littéraire*, Arles: ATLAS, 191-207.

———, 1995. *The Search for the Perfect Language*, translated by James Fentress. Oxford, Cambridge: Blackwell.

Edelman, Murray, 1971. *Politics as Symbolic Action. Mass Arousal and Quiescence*. Chicago: Markham.

Elghezouani, Abdelhak, 2007. Professionalisation of interpreters. The case of mental health care. *In:* Cecilia Wadensjö, Birgitta Englund Dimitrova & Anna-Lena Nilsson, eds. *The Critical Link 4. Professionalisation of interpreting in the community*. Amsterdam, Philadelphia: John Benjamins, 215-225.

Eriten, Nilüfer Duygu & Jennifer Romine, 1994. Instrumental and Symbolic Sources of Ethnic Conflict: Application to the Kurdish Conflict in Turkey. *In:* Eric Jan Zurcher, ed. *Turkey: A Modern History*. London: St Martin's Press, 1-44.

European Commission, 2017. Countering online hate speech – Commission initiative with social media platforms and civil society shows progress, Brussels: European Commission. Online: http://europa.eu/rapid/press-release_IP-17-1471_en.htm.

Faiola, Anthony, 2016. Germany Springs to Action over Hate Speech Against Migrants, *Washington Post*. Online: https://www.washingtonpost.com/world/europe/germany-springs-to-action-over-hate-speech-against-migrants/2016/01/06/6031218e-b315-11e5-8abc-d09392edc612_story.html.

Fioretti, Julia & Foo Y. Chee, 2016. Facebook, Twitter, YouTube, Microsoft Back EU Hate Speech Rules, *REUTERS*, May 31. Online: http://www.reuters.com/article/us-eu-facebook-twitter-hatecrime-idUSKCN0YM0VJ.

Fishman, Joshua, 1986. Bilingualism and Separatism. *Annals of the American Academy of Political and Social Sciences (AAPSS)*, 487, 169-180.

Floros, Georgios, 2012. News Translation and Translation Ethics in the Cypriot Context. *Meta*, 57(4), 924-942.

Freedman, Harry & Maurice Simon, eds., 1939. *Rabba Genesis (Middrash Rabbah)*, Hertford: Stephen Austin & Sons.

Gadamer, Hans Georg, 1960. *Wahrheit und Methode. Grundzüge einer philosophischen Hermeneutik*. Tübingen: Mohr.

Giddens, Anthony, 1977. Review: Habermas's Social and Political Theory. *The American Journal of Sociology*, 83(1), 198-212.

Glazer, Nathan & Daniel Patrick Moynihan, 1963. *Beyond the Melting Pot*. Cambridge: The M.I.T. Press, Harvard UniversityPress.

Gomes de Andrade, Norberto Nuno, 2005. Enhanced Cooperation: the Ultimate Challenge of Managing Diversity in Europe. *Intereconomics*, 40(4), 201-216.

Grigoriadis, Ioannis N., 2018. *Democratic Transition and the Rise of Populist Majoritarianism. Constitutional Reform in Greece and Turkey*. Cham: Palgrave Macmillan.

Habermas, Jürgen, 1992. *Faktizität und Geltung. Beiträge zur Diskurstheorie des Rechts und des demokratischen Rechtsstaats*. Frankfurt am Main: Suhrkamp.

Haidt, Jonathan, 2001. The Emotional Dog and Its Rational Tail: A Social Intuitionist Approach to Moral Judgment. *Psychological Review*, 108(4), 814-834.

———, 2007. The New Synthesis in Moral Psychology. *Science*, 316, 998-1002.

———, 2012. *The Righteous Mind: Why Good People Are Divided by Politics and Religion*. Vintage Books.

Haller, Max & Markus Hadler, 2006. How social relations and structures can produce happiness and unhapiness: An international comparative analysis. *Social Indicators Research*, 75, 169-216.

Harvey, Andy, 2012. Regulating homophobic hate speech: Back to basics about language and politics? *Sexualities*, 15(2), 191-206.

He, Baogan, Brian Galligan & Takashi Inoguchi, eds., 2007. *Federalism in Asia*, Cheltenham: Edward Elgar.

Heider, Fritz, 1958. *The Psychology of Interpersonal Relations*. New York: John Wiley & Sons.

Heilbron, Johan & Gisèle Sapiro, 2002. Traduction: les échanges littéraires internationaux, *Actes de la recherche en sciences sociales*.

Henson, Billy, Bradford W. Reyns & Bonnie S. Fisher, 2013. Fear of crime online? Examining the effect of risk, previous victimization, and exposure on fear of online interpersonal victimization. *Journal of Contemporary Criminal Justice*, 29(4), 475-497.

Hinduja, Sameer & Justin W. Patchin, 2007. Offline Consequences of Online Victimization. *Journal of School Violence*, 6(3), 89-112. Online: http://dx.doi.org/10.1300/J202v06n03_06.

Hitchens, Christopher, 2011. *The Enemy*. Amazon.

Hughes, Claretha, 2014. *American Black Women and Interpersonal Leadership Styles*. Rotterdam: Sense Publishers.

———, 2016. *Diversity Intelligence. Integrating Diversity Intelligence alongside Intellectual, Emotional, and Cultural Intelligence for Leadership and Career Development*. New York: Palgrave Macmillan.

Hung, Eva, ed. 2005. *Translation and cultural change studies in history, norms and image-projection*, Amsterdam, Philadelphia: John Benjamins.

Inghilleri, Moira, 2003. Habitus, Field and Discourse: Interpreting as a socially situated activity. *Target*, 15(2), 243-268.

———, 2010. You Don't Make War Without Knowing Why. The Decision to Interpret in Iraq. *The Translator*, 16(2), 175-196.

Inghilleri, Moira & Sue-Ann Harding, 2010. Translating violent conflict. *The Translator*, 16, 165-173.

Johnson, Allan G., 2006. *Privilege, power, and difference*. 2 ed. New York: McGraw Hill.

Jupp, Victor, Pamela Davies & Peter Francis, 1999. The Features of Invisible Crimes. *In:* Pamela Davies, Peter Francis & Victor Jupp, eds. *Invisible Crimes. Their victims and their regulation*. New York: Macmillan, 3-28.

Kaufman, Stuart J., 2001. *Modern Hatreds. The Symbolic Politics of Ethnic Wars*. Ithaca, London: Cornell University Press.

Kazal, Russell A., 1995. Revisiting assimilation: The rise, fall, and reappraisal of a concept in American ethnic history. *The American Historical Review*, 100(2), 437-471.

Ladmiral, Jean-René, 2004. Babel & Logos. *Forum*, 2(2), 1-28.

Lash, Scott & Mike Featherstone, 2002. Recognition and Difference. *In:* Scott Lash & Mike Featherstone, eds. *Recognition and Difference: Politics, Identity, Multiculture*. London: Sage, 1-19.

Leanza, Yvan, 2007. Roles of community interpreters in pediatrics as seen by interpreters, physicians and researchers. *In:* Franz Pöchhacker & Miriam Shlesinger, eds. *Healthcare Interpreting. Discourse and Interaction*. Amsterdam, Philadelphia: John Benjamins, 11-34.

Lefevere, André, ed. 1992. *Translation/History/Culture. A Sourcebook*, London, New York: Routledge.

Levene, Mark, 2000. Why Is the Twentieth Century the Century of Genocide? *Journal of World History*, 11(2), 305-336.

Lipton, G., M. Arends, K. Bastian, B. Wright & P. O'Hara, 2002. The psychosocial consequences experienced by interpreters in relation to working with torture and trauma clients: A West Australian pilot study. *Synergy*, Winter, 3-13.

López Guix, Juan Gabriel, 2007. Tras la sombra de Babel. *1611*, 1. Online: http://www.traduccionliteraria.org/1611/art/lopezguix.htm.

MacFarlane, A., Z. Dzebisova, D. Karapish, B. Kovacevic, F. Ogbebor & E. Okonkwo, 2009. Arranging and negotiating the use of informal interpreters in general practice consultations: experiences of refugees and asylum seekers in the west of Ireland. *Social Science and Medicine*, 69(2), 210-214. Online: http://www.ncbi.nlm.nih.gov/pubmed/19535192.

de Man, Paul, 1991. Conclusions : « La Tâche du traducteur » de Walter Benjamin. *TTR: Traduction, terminologie, rédaction*, 4(2), 21-52.

Mason, Gail, 2013. The symbolic purpose of hate crime law: Ideal victims and emotion. *Theoretical Criminology*, 18(1), 75-92.

Merlini, Raffaela, 2009. Seeking asylum and seeking identity in a mediated encounter. The projection of selves through discursive practices. *Interpreting*, 11(1), 57-92.

Mucchi-Faina, Angelica, Sandro Costarelli & Chiara Romoli, 2002. The effects of intergroup context of evaluation on ambivalence toward the ingroup and the outgroup. *European Journal of Social Psychology*, 32(2), 247-259.

Niska, Helge, 1995. Just Interpreting: Role Conflicts and Discourse Types in Court Interpreting. *In:* Marshall Morris, ed. *Translation and the Law.* Amsterdam, Philadelphia: John Benjamins, 293-316.

Nosek, Brian A., 2007. Implicit-explicit relations. *Current Directions in Psychological Science,* 16, 65-69.

Oakeshott, Michael, 1962. The Tower of Babel. *Rationalism in Politics and other essays.* London: Methuen & Co., 59-79.

Palmer, Jerry, 2007. Interpreters and Translators on the Front Line. Interpreting and Translation for Western Media in Iraq. *In:* Myriam Salama-Carr, ed. *Translating and Interpreting Conflict.* Amsterdam, New York: Rodopi, 13-28.

Parekh, Bhikhu, 2005. Hate speech. Is there a case for banning? *Public Policy Research,* December 2005-February 2006, 213-223.

Park, Augustine S. J., 2010. Peacebuilding, the Rule of Law and the Problem of Culture: Assimilation, Multiculturalism, Deployment. *Journal of Intervention and Statebuilding,* 4(4), 413-432.

Peled, Yael & Matteo Bonotti, 2016. Tongue-Tied: Rawls, Political Philosophy and Metalinguistic Awareness. *American Political Science Review,* 110(04), 798-811.

Plous, Scott, 2003. The Psychology of Prejudice, Stereotyping and Discrimination: An Overview. *In:* Scott Plous, ed. *Understanding Prejudice and Discrimination.* New York: McGraw-Hill, 3-48.

Pöllabauer, Sonja, 2004. Interpreting in asylum hearings: Issues of role, responsibility and power. *Interpreting,* 6(2), 143-180.

———, 2008. Forschung zum Dolmetschen im Asylverfahren: Interdisziplinarität und Netzwerke. *Lebende Sprachen,* 53(3), 121-129.

Postmes, Tom & Laura G. E. Smith, 2009. Why Do the Privileged Resort to Oppression? A Look at Some Intragroup Factors. *Journal of Social Issues,* 65(4), 769-790.

Prunč, Erich, 2004. Zum Objektbereich der Translationswissenschaft. *In:* Ina Müller, ed. *Und sie bewegt sich doch... Translationswissenschaft in Ost und West. Festschrift für Heidemarie Salevsky zum 60. Geburtstag.* Frankfurt: Peter Lang, 263-285.

Puig i Ferreter, Joan, 1975. *Diari d'un escriptor: ressonàncies, 1942-1952.* Barcelona: Edicions 62.

Rawls, John, 1971. *A Theory of Justice.* Cambridge: Harvard University Press.

Rodoreda, Mercè, 1974. *Mirall trencat.* Barcelona: Club Editor.

Rubini, Monica, Silvia Moscatelli & Augusto Palmonari, 2016. Increasing Group Entitativity. *Group Processes & Intergroup Relations,* 10(2), 280-296.

Scanlon, Thomas Michael, 2003. *The Difficulty of Tolerance: Essays in Political Philosophy.* Cambridge, New York: Cambridge University Press.

Schneider, David J., 2003. *The Psychology of Stereotyping.* New York, London: The Guilford Press.

Schöpflin, George, 1997. The Functions of Myth and a Taxonomy of Myths. *In:* Geoffrey Hoskins & George Schöpflin, eds. *Myths and Nationhood.* London: C. Hurst & Co., 19-35.

Sen, Amartya, 1980. Equality of What? *In:* Sterling Mcmurrin, ed. *Tanner Lectures on Human Values*. Cambridge, Salt Lake City: Cambridge University Press, University of Utah Press, 195-220.

———, 2009. *The Idea of Justice*. Cambridge, MA: The Belknap Press.

Singh, Anita Inder, 1995. Managing National Diversity through Political Structures and Ideologies: The Soviet Experience in Comparative Perspective. *Nations and Nationalism*, 1(2), 197-220.

Smith, Eliot R. & Jamie DeCoster, 2000. Dual-Process Models in Social and Cognitive Psychology: Conceptual Integration and Links to Underlying Memory Systems. *Personality and Social Psychology Review*, 4, 108-131.

Spencer, Steven J., Steven Fein, Connie T. Wolfe, Chistina Fong & Meghan A. Dunn, 1998. Automatic Activation of Stereotypes: The role of self-image threat. *Personality and Social Psychology Bulletin*, 24, 1139–1152.

Sporer, Siegfried Ludwig, 2001. Recognizing Faces of Other Ethnic Groups: An integration of theories. *Psychology, Public Policy, and Law*, 7(1), 36-97.

Stahuljak, Zrinka, 2010. War, Translation, Transnationalism: Interpreters in and of the war (Croatia, 1991-1992). *In:* Mona Baker, ed. *Critical Readings in Translation Studies*. 391-414.

Steiner, George, 1975. *After Babel: Aspects of Language and Translation*. London: Oxford University Press.

Strachan, Glenda, John Burgess & Anne Sullivan, 2004. Affirmative action or managing diversity: what is the future of equal opportunity policies in organisations? *Women in Management Review*, 19(4), 196-204.

Strack, Fritz & Roland Deutsch, 2004. Reflective and impulsive determinants of social behavior. *Personality and Social Psychology Review*, 8, 220-247.

Stychin, Carl F., 2004. Same-Sex Sexualities and the Globalization of Human Rights Discourse. *McGill Law Journal*, 49, 951-968.

Tajfel, Henri & Michael Billic, 1974. Familiarity and categorization in intergroup behavior. *Journal of Experimental Social Psychology*, 10(2), 110-170.

Tajfel, Henri & John C. Turner, 1979. An integrative theory of intergroup conflict. *In:* William G. Austin & Stephen Worchel, eds. *The social psychology of intergroup relations*. Monterey: Brooks, Cole, 33-47.

Thompson, Allan, ed. 2007. *The Media and the Rwanda Genocide*, London, Ann Arbor: Pluto Press.

Toggenburg, Gabriel N., 2005. Who is Managing Ethnic and Cultural Diversity in the European Condominium? The Moments of Entry, Integration and Preservation. *Journal of Common Market Studies*, 43(4), 717-738.

Tymoczko, Maria, 2006. Translation: Ethics, Ideology, Action. *The Massachusetts Review*, 47, 442-461.

———, 2007. *Enlarging Translation, Empowering Translators*. Manchester & Kinderhook: St. Jerome.

UNESCO General Conference (United Nations Educational, Scientific and Cultural Organization), 2005. Convention on the Protection and Promotion of the Diversity of Cultural Expressions, Paris. Online: http://unesdoc.unesco.org/images/0014/001429/142919e.pdf.

UNGA (United Nations General Assembly), 1948. Universal Declaration of Human Rights, Resolution 217A (III), United Nations Treaties Series Paris. Online: http://www.un.org/en/universal-declaration-human-rights/.

Valdeón, Roberto A., 2013. Doña Marina/La Malinche: A historiographical approach to the interpreter/traitor. *Target*, 25, 157-179.

Veenstra, Kristine & S. Alexander Haslam, 2000. Willingness to participate in industrial protest: Exploring social identification in context. *British Journal of Social Psychology*, 39(1), 153-172.

Veltkamp, Martijn, Henk Aarts & Ruud Custers, 2008. Perception in the Service of Goal Pursuit: Motivation to Attain Goals Enhances the Perceived Size of Goal-Instrumental Objects. *Social Cognition*, 26(6), 720-736.

Venuti, Lawrence, 1998. *The Scandals of Translation. Towards an ethics of difference*. London: Routledge.

Verkuyten, Maykel, 2005. Ethnic group identification and group evaluation among minority and majority groups: testing the multiculturalism hypothesis. *Journal of personality and social psychology*, 88(1), 121-138.

———, 2009. Self-esteem and multiculturalism: An examination among ethnic minority and majority groups in the Netherlands. *Journal of Research in Personality*, 43(3), 419-427.

———, 2010. Assimilation ideology and situational well-being among ethnic minority members. *Journal of Experimental Social Psychology*, 46(2), 269-275.

Vertovec, Steven, 2010. Towards post-multiculturalism? Changing communities, conditions and contexts of diversity. *International Social Science Journal*, 61(199), 83-95.

Weigert, Andrew J., Joyce Smith Teitge & Dennis W. Teitge, 1986. *Society and identity: Toward a sociological psychology*. Cambridge: Cambridge University Press.

Williams, Robin M., 1947. *The reduction of intergroup tension*. New York: Social Science Research Council.

Wills, Thomas Ashby, 1981. Downward Comparison Principles in Social Psychology. *Psychological Bulletin*, 90(2), 245-271.

———, 1990. Similarity and self-esteem in downward comparison. In: Jerry Suls & Thomas Ashby Wills, eds. *Social Comparison: Contemporary Theory and Research*. Hillsdale: Lawrence Erlbaum, 51-78.

Wilson, Timothy D., 2002. *Strangers to Ourselves: Discovering the Adaptive Unconscious*. Cambridge: Belknap Press.

Winter, Jay & Michael Teitelbaum, 2013. *The Global Spread of Fertility Decline: Population, Fear, and Uncertainty*. New Haven, London: Yale University Press.

Wolf, Michaela, 1999. Zum Sozialen Sinn in der Translation. *Arcadia*, 34(2), 262-273.

Wolsko, Christopher, Bernadette Park & Charles M. Judd, 2006. Considering the Tower of Babel: Correlates of Assimilation and Multiculturalism among Ethnic Minority and Majority Groups in the United States. *Social Justice Research*, 19(3), 277-306.

Wright, Robert, 2009. *The Evolution of God.* New York: Little, Brown and Company.
Wright, Stephen C., Arthur Aron, Tracy McLaughlin-Volpe & Stacy A. Ropp, 1997. The Extended Contact Effect: Knowledge of Cross-Group Friendships and Prejudice. *Journal of Personality and Social Psychology,* 73(1), 73-90.
Zajonc, Robert B., 1980. Feeling and Thinking: Preferences Need no Inference. *American Psychologist,* 35, 151-175.
Zangwill, Israel, 1925. The Melting Pot: A Drama in Four Acts. *The Works of Israel Zangwill.* London: The Globe Publishing Co., 30-31.
Zbarauskaitė, Asta, Neringa Grigutytė & Danute Gailienė, 2015. Minority Ethnic Identity and Discrimination Experience in a Context of Social Transformations. *Procedia - Social and Behavioral Sciences,* 165(6), 121-130.
Zick, Andreas, Beate Küpper & Andreas Hövermann, 2011. *Intolerance, Prejudice and Discrimination. A European Report,* Berlin: Friedrich Ebert Stiftung. Online: http://library.fes.de/pdf-files/do/07908-20110311.pdf.

Chapter 3

Unveiling and redressing inequality dynamics in legal and institutional translation: from symbolic violence to symbolic recognition

Rosario Martín Ruano

Institutional discourse often depicts translation as a safeguard of the egalitarian ideals that multilingualism purportedly guarantees, as an activity of prime importance in the development of healthy multicultural and diverse societies. However, it well may be the case that, in the prevailing globalized, asymmetrically multicultural order where various forms of multilingualism coexist, long-standing legal and institutional translation practices may be contributing, albeit involuntarily, to engendering or perpetuating unequal relations of hegemony and subordination between dominant cultures and powers, and minoritized languages and identities. Drawing on the concept of recognition, this article problematizes the equation linking translation-mediated multilingualism with egalitarianism. A number of factors which accentuate translation's potential proclivity to exercise symbolic violence in our day and age are identified: prevailing professional narratives and practices shaping legal and institutional translators as conduits; centripetal language and translation ideologies promoting uniformity to the detriment of diversity; the impact of the pivotal role of English and its influence over minority languages in the communicative fluxes of our global era, and the revival of literalism fostered by increasingly automated translation practices.

Introduction

As can be seen in the discourse propagated by a variety of institutions in our day and age, translation is often portrayed as an activity of prime importance in the development and progress of healthy multicultural and diverse societies, as a safeguard of the egalitarian ideals multilingualism purportedly guarantees – i.e., ensuring the sameness of languages and citizens before the institution and before the law, and recognizing, respecting and enhancing language and cultural difference (Wagner et al. 2002; Sosoni 2005). However, despite the seemingly indisputable correlation between multilingualism (aided by translation) and (linguistic) equality which can be found in political statements by certain institutions and in dominant narratives both in the social and political arena *and* in (legal) translation studies, neither the linguistic landscapes of our day and age nor currently existing language and translation institutional strategies can be easily or straightforwardly understood, explained and theorized in terms of *horizontal* relations between languages. Rosello's (2012) confrontation of EU's multilingual policy with Europe's plurilingual reality is revealing in this regard. Rosello highlights the sheer differences between "the dream of a constellation of equal languages" promoted at institutional level, often with the assistance of translation, and the "messy but productive constellation that is made up of overlaps, discrepancies and incomplete forms of multilingualism that produce shifting power relationships between Europeans" (2012, p. 215) which exists on the ground. Furthermore, by contrasting the "visual symbolic space" created by an institutional EU webpage which lists all EU official languages associated to their corresponding flags with other phenomena which become overshadowed by this image – the "minority" and "migrant" languages that are excluded from the list, the "irregular traffic that takes place between languages", the spaces of "intersection, intercomprehension and creolization" among languages, and "the fact that territorial and linguistic borders do not coincide" (2012, p. 220-221) –, Rosello shows the limitations and shortcomings of the dominant panegyric narrative on multilingualism in which translation is often invoked as a key tool working at the service of *equality*.

Of course, this is not to deny the potentiality of translation to promote multiculturalism and inclusivity. Indeed, translation is often actively used as an instrument through which societies decide to deliberately display their plurality. Meylaerts (2011) establishes a typology of prototypical linguistic and translational territoriality regimes to categorize the policies adopted by authorities to communicate with multilingual populations. Even if, according to Meylaerts, "most contemporary democratic societies seem to opt for a monolingual territoriality regime tempered by more or less extensive translation services for their territorial and/or immigrant minorities" (2011, p. 753), the very adoption of a multilingual communication policy implies and shows a will on the part of authorities to recognize, at least to a certain extent, linguistic and cultural difference as a constitutive societal factor. Monzó (2017, p. 113) also observes that translation and interpreting are actively used for achieving higher levels of ethnolinguistic democracy in the current "linguascape of international organisations," which nevertheless reveals a significant underrepresentation of minority cultures. By contrast, the absence of translation in plurilingual organizations or societies might be extremely telling: although it is often highly dependent on the prestige of the languages involved, it might also be indicative of – or be construed as – an exclusionary strategy providing political support to a particular language option and to a particular ideology towards diversity to the detriment of certain constituencies. This became evident in the reactions triggered by the disappearance of Spanish language content from the White House website shortly after Donald Trump's inauguration as US president in January 2017, which was commented upon internationally (Couzens 2017; O'Keefe 2017). Even when the unavailability of the Spanish version of the official webpage might have been a side-effect of lack of foresight of the new administration, it was internationally portrayed as "un portazo a la comunidad hispana de Estados Unidos"[1] (Ayuso 2017). In any event, for the purposes of this article, it is important to underline that the links between translation, multilingualism and the promotion of equality are complex. In order to gain a better understanding of the role played by translation in institutional settings, deconstructing the direct, triangular correlation often established among these three elements might be both relevant and enlightening. A first factor that is to be taken into account is that, as Castro, Mainer and Page (2017, p. 1) remind us, "[b]e it within Europe or elsewhere, one of the aspects of multilingualism is a power differential between languages." Furthermore, it may well be the case that long-standing translation practices in the legal and institutional fields may be contributing, albeit perhaps involuntarily, to generating or to perpetuating unequal relations of hegemony and subordination among powers, cultures, languages and identities. By adopting a critical stance which might help to shed light on the cracks and contradictions in this tripartite connection, the purpose of these pages is to contribute to the articulation of more inclusive and equitable translation practice models which might be more prepared to respond to the challenges of pluralism and to allow for the expression of the nuances of diversity.

Translation and multilingualism(s)

The seemingly indisputable connection among translation, multilingualism and equality becomes unsteady inasmuch as, as argued by authors including Blommaert and Rampton (2011), Blommaert (2013) or Moreno Cabrera (2016), multilingualism is a polyhedral, multifaceted phenomenon in the

---

[1] "A slamming of the door in the face of the US Hispanic community" (author's translation).

complex contemporary social landscapes of our global era, characterized by frequent language contact. In fact, as Karpinski (2015) highlights, multilingualism must be conceived of in the plural, as there are many, and very varied, types of multilingualism coexisting in our societies. In relation to individual multilingual behavior, Moreno Cabrera (2016) establishes a distinction between modalities of synthetic and analytical plurilingualism – the first featuring a capacity of users to actively employ different languages, and the second restricted to their capacity to process and to understand them in a passive way –, as well as different responses to diglossic situations, including forms of *code-switching, code-blending* and *language intertwining* occurrences with varying degrees of the *matrix* or *host language* and the *embedded language*. Similarly, Blommaert and Rampton (2011, p. 7) compile a myriad of labels differentiating behavioral patterns adopted by multilingual individuals, including *languaging, polylanguaging, heteroglossia, crossing, metrolingualism,* etc. Lantto (2016) completes this taxonomy with other categories, including *borrowing, nonce-borrowing, code-alternation, code-mixing, translanguaging, codemeshing,* etc.

In addition to idiosyncratic patterns shown by multilingual individuals, Moreno Cabrera (2016, p. 173 ff.) observes that there are different types of social multilingualisms which generate a wide variety of interactive relations between the behavior of plurilingual or monolingual individuals and the language choices adopted institutionally at a social level in a specific context. Moreno Cabrera explains that, depending on the support for or resistance against multilingualism existing at an institutional level, authorities might either contribute to language preservation or boost language shift or displacement –and ultimately, the replacement or disappearance of a language. When assessed in the social reality, multilingualism does not necessarily elicit the unfailingly positive view in the mainstream laudatory discourse in institutional settings of our day and age. Conversely, it might be interpreted in a very different manner depending on the social prestige of the languages involved. In an already classical study on languages in America, Dicker (1996) observed that prestige forms of multilingualism coexisted with plebeian ones. Depending on the social reputation of a given language, native speakers feel prone to maintain their mother tongue and showcase it as an important asset or, to the contrary, decide to renounce it and hide it to avoid the perception of this language as an obstacle to integration, assimilation, and social success. Similarly, Karpinski (2015, p. 28) makes a useful distinction between "multilingualism 'from above,'" linked to economic privilege, free mobility, and commodity exchange" and "multilingualism 'from below,' associated with pre-modern temporality, non-marketability, and invisibility." Karpinski also draws on the terminology proposed by Noorani to note that both situations of "soft" multilingualism and "hard" multilingualism are experienced at a social level today (Karpinski 2015, p. 31). In the first case, language contact takes place in a shared reference frame which approximates the reality of plurilingual settings to monolingual regimes; in the second case, multilingualism lays bare the sharp edges of difference, as well as a feeling of incommensurability and lack of intelligibility.

For the purposes of this article, it is important to highlight that legal and institutional translation operates today in extremely heterogeneous multilingual settings, in which it adopts a wide range of different practices aligned with particular forms of multilingualism. For this reason, neither is it possible to reflect on translation in the singular in our current order of multiple and kaleidoscopic multilingualisms. Rather, our time is characterized by the coexistence of diverse translation models resulting in similarly diverse implications. In this regard, the translation model selected will inevitably favor a specific formula for the management of identities and of cultural difference, thus committing itself with a given regime vis-à-vis alterity to the detriment of other possibilities.

In this regard, translation in general, and legal and institutional translation in particular, contributes in a crucial and decisive manner to the construction of a particular symbolic order where the borders between social and cultural identities will be either further demarcated and reinforced or erased. This becomes evident, in the first place, when legal and institutional translation is analyzed at the macro-level, in terms of selection policies. The actual decision on which languages will be accorded "official" status at a given moment in a particular institutional frame – i.e., on which will be the target languages in a given action or in the multilingual communication policy of an international or a national institution – often entails privileging certain cultural identities over others with which they coexist and/or collide. In a chapter significantly entitled "European Elites: Official Languages in the EU", Craith (2006) examines the processes and implications behind the successive addition of EU working languages following the accession of different countries, which required or involved constructing linguistic differences between what were thus far considered to be proximate language varieties, dismissing the status of official, working language at EU level for certain languages that were co-official at national level or negotiating a special status for other languages that were indeed co-official at national level, but which would have been overburdened by a similar status at EU level. What is more, the selection of a relevant target language proves to be an even more complex and sensitive issue if we take into account that our era has been defined, following Vertovec (2007), as that of "super-diversity", a term which attempts to reflect the "diversification of diversity" in our contemporary societies. In social spaces which bear witness to "increasingly stratified and multiple processes and effects of migration, leading to heightened complexity" and where ever "more people – from more varied cultural and linguistic backgrounds, subject to more varied conditions of mobility and legal status – come into regular contact with one another in today's growing cities" (Vertovec 2015, p. 1), the choice of target languages by an institution implies granting visibility and legitimacy to certain cultural identities, but most probably to the exclusion of other communities. From this point of view, translation and interpreting emerge as key instruments in the current geopolitical language economy and dynamics.

Secondly, legal and institutional translation also contribute to the construction of particular symbolic orders at a micro-level, in their linguistic or textual realization. As Hermans (1999, p. 95) argued in relation to every translated text, a legal or institutional translated text may also be considered to be an index of self-definition. The choices it performs at many levels reveal how a (legal) culture perceives itself in contrast with the other culture or cultures involved – as Lambert (2013, p. 261) reminds us, binary relations have often been superseded by multilateral relations in the current global scenario. Firstly, the actual selection of a text or a type of texts to be translated into a given language by an institution may be a strategic move in the symbolic space where identity issues are addressed and negotiated. When inquiring into what is translated and into the underlying causes for or purposes of certain legal and institutional translation commissions, it becomes evident that legal and institutional translation is not always driven by informational demands but may predominantly fulfill symbolic functions and meet identitarian needs. Koskinen (2000) coins the term "existential equivalence" to refer to (legal and institutional) translations which may be considered to be redundant from the point of view of their communicative usefulness, and the significance of which lies in their very existence. Secondly, inasmuch as a translation unavoidably needs to select a distinctive language norm and tradition, it takes a specific stance on existing conventions and expectations. In this regard, translation will forcibly choose between major and minor languages, or at least between major or minor uses and options within a particular major or minor language (Venuti 1998a). To the extent that, in our era, the evolution of any language necessarily entails both a reaction to the predominance of English as a *lingua franca* or pivot language in many transfer processes and to other languages with which it may have multifaceted neighborly relations, any legal or institutional translation today creates a particular balance between the global and the local. Acting at the linguistic and symbolic level, translation plays a key part, in a very particular manner, in search of the ever-contingent and renewable agreements which are the formulae of social coexistence. From a perspective which locates translation within the asymmetrical dynamics of globalization and within the networks woven by the affinities and tensions among languages, cultures and identities, legal and institutional translation – *every* instance of legal and institutional translation – therefore emerges as a political and inevitably politicized act. From this point of view, no legal or institutional translation can posit itself as neither neutral nor innocent. In this regard, legal and institutional translation is involved in the construction of the present – a particular present – in which the inherited relations among collectivities are updated and where a particular paradigm for the future is envisaged from a specific standpoint which outlines an actual horizon for the expression of plurality. Either involuntarily or deliberately, legal and institutional translation takes part in the performative negotiation of shared meanings and of the differences as perceived and tolerated among various identities – in the *recognition* of the mutable borders between Self and Other. *Recognition* proves to be a pertinent notion for problematizing the implications of legal and institutional translation.

Legal and institutional translation, redistribution and recognition

In recent decades, the principles which should serve as the foundation for justice and, more precisely, of social justice have been the object of intense debate in the field of legal studies and political theory. One of the most productive debates has opposed – in an excessively Manichean way, according to some authors – the concepts of redistribution and recognition. It is our contention that the discussion around these concepts might be extrapolated to the field of legal and institutional translation in order to shed light on, and ultimately address, the shortcomings of dominant translation models in legal and institutional settings.

Authors associated with the "recognition paradigm" raise the relevance of posing an alternative to the concept of "redistribution" which, in their opinion, can be considered to have been traditionally inspiring solutions for combatting inequalities among various social groups and identities. In this regard, the redistributive paradigm addresses perceived disadvantages with corrective measures designed to ensure the same rights and opportunities for every individual or identity, regardless of the idiosyncrasies of the target community. Redistribution, in its commitment to evenness, presupposes and searches for sameness as an ideal. In the opinion of its critics, this willingness to redress the unequal standing of differentiated social groups with identical treatment brings about the disregard and contempt of diversity and the neutralizing of specificities in difference-blind actions.

It could be argued that, to a large extent, translation policies implemented at the service of multilingualism in legal and institutional settings are ultimately inspired by or justified according to a redistributive logic. Merely by way of illustration, a recurrent element in the narrative script activated in relation to the co-official languages in the European Union invokes the need to ensure the same rights to all citizens of the Union, the underlying narrative assumption being that, in the absence of institutional documents in their language, certain citizens would be disadvantaged if deprived of their right to information and direct communication with the institution. Needless to say, this mental image projected by the narrative which conceptualizes translation as a remedial action obscures the delicate negotiations and complex political and economic factors behind the recognition of official status for certain languages, the denial of this recognition for other ones or even the refusal of authorities to put forward such demand in other cases. Furthermore, it both relies on and reinforces the monoglot and monocultural paradigm which mistakenly takes for granted monolingualism as a norm.

In addition to this, the dominant translation model applied in order to ensure this right repeatedly invoked is frequently also inspired by the principle of equality-as-sameness which underlies redistributive models: studies on translation in the European Union have demonstrated the predominance of what Venuti (1998b, p. 82) calls an *ethics of sameness* in institutional translation – i.e., translation strategies favoring a visible but misleading identicalness. Indeed, on the grounds that equivalence in institutional settings is attained through the promotion of similarities at surface-level which, in fact, do not take into account the profound differences separating languages and cultural traditions, Koskinen (2000) describes the hegemonic translation paradigm in institutional settings as a "chimera" or an "institutional illusion". While Koskinen analyzes this phenomenon in the context of the EU by focusing on the case of a minority language such as Finnish, which has an autochthonous tradition of drafting legislation which is close to the citizen, according to Šarčević, this also applies to the case of English, inasmuch as "terminology and drafting style [in the EU] are shaped by the continental legal tradition and Romance language influence" (Šarčević 2015, p. 9). In this regard, despite the formal similitude among authenticated versions, translated texts produced according to the concept of equivalence understood as "linguistic concordance" which is dominant in the EU (Strandvik 2002, p. 461) may in fact be the source of varying degrees of identification and/or feelings of alienation in diverse legal cultures at different points in time.

The concept of "recognition", as inspired by the ideas of authors including Taylor (1994), Honneth (1995), Fraser (2002), and Fraser and Honneth (2003), has been called for as an alternative foundation against the redistributive paradigm and for the attainment of social justice in the field of political theory. Whereas redistribution worships equality as an ideal, recognition, on the contrary, emphasizes the value of diversity, i.e. differences in the cultural and symbolic dimension (Lash and Featherstone 2002, p. 2-3). Indeed, the notion of recognition has been extremely inspirational in contemporary debates on and in approaches to *multiculturalism*, which, in addition to being a feature of our contemporary cultures, is also, most importantly, an unresolved challenge and an ongoing, never-ending undertaking for globalized societies. Taking into account that many different conceptualizations, readings, and projects of multiculturalism do exist, albeit often contradictory ones, increasingly ethnically-, linguistically-, and culturally-diverse societies need to find their own particular versions of socially-accepted and institutionally-promoted multiculturalism. Indeed, possibilities range, among others, from the purportedly well-intentioned politics of "integration", still a buzz word in the discourses of many diverse societies –a word which often entails an asymmetrical, unilateral demand placed solely upon non-hegemonic groups to blend into an imaginary standard where they will probably never be seen to belong–; to the "shallow global diversity approach", which merely enlarges prevailing canons with the anecdotal presence of the margins, and which Friedman (1995: 14) perceives as opposed to a concept of "deep multiculturalism", in which both dominant and minority groups question their own assumptions; and the "citizenization multiculturalism" proposed by Kymlicka (2010) as an alternative to a superficial and fetishistic multiculturalism which venerates exotic elements but which does not interrogate the deficits in equality that exist among groups in plural societies. Indeed, in the recognition paradigm, *equality* is not conceived as the pursuit of *sameness* in a universal way, as if every subject or community would and should be identical to any other, but rather as the understanding and appreciation of their idiosyncrasies and singularities. In this regard, the value of diversity is reassessed and emphasized. To put it with an oft-quoted statement by Taylor (1994, p. 26), "[d]ue recognition is not a courtesy that we owe people. It is a basic human need".

Perceiving that inequalities are frequently brought about or exacerbated in subtle subordination dynamics which disregard, undervalue or stigmatize the specificities of certain identities, Nancy Fraser (in Fraser and Honneth 2003, p. 13) highlights the importance of combatting hierarchies which become evident and perpetuated in social patterns of *representation, interpretation* and *communication,* by which unequal value or capacity is recognized and conferred to certain communities or actors which are constituted "as inferior, excluded, wholly other, or simply invisible — in other words, as less than full partners in social interaction" (Fraser 2000, p. n/p). Needless to say, research in translation studies has repeatedly drawn attention to the risk that translation may align itself with existing powers and dominant ideologies and misrepresent certain groups, even if and when it may be supposedly undertaken to speak for these groups (Niranjana 1992; Bassnett and Lefevere 1998; House et al. 2005; Cronin 2006). For the purposes of this article, Cronin's (1995) reflection on the dual and paradoxical interrelations between translation and minority languages are particularly relevant. Cronin perceives that, in these contexts, translation may be both an asset and a useful tool for visibility, and yet also a potential danger – a deliberate or involuntary accomplice in the alteration or neglect of the specificity of minorities, in their subjugation to hegemonic patterns and mainstream views, and in the adulteration of their singularities under the influence of the interests or perceptions of major players. In order to counteract the self-reinforcing mechanisms of inequality, Fraser encourages intervention in the institutionalized practices which legitimize power differentials and the subversion of the representational regimes by which certain identities are excluded, made invisible, dehumanized or stereotyped, and thus denied their self-realization and involvement as full members in the construction and redefinition of social reality on a par with the identities reified as the *norm*. According to Fraser (Fraser 2002, p. 24, 29), the goal of "participatory parity" should be pursued in actions inspired by recognition politics.

In our opinion, Fraser's ideas are of great interest for translation in general – a practice requiring and involved in *representation, interpretation* and *communication* tasks – and, particularly, for translation in legal and institutional settings. Fraser expressly refers to these settings when explaining the variety of forms which misrecognition can assume:

> In today's complex, differentiated societies, parity-impeding values are institutionalized at a plurality of institutional sites, and in qualitatively different modes. In some cases, misrecognition is juridified, expressly codified in formal law; in other cases, it is institutionalized via government policies, administrative codes or professional practice. It can also be institutionalized informally—in associational patterns, longstanding customs or sedimented social practices of civil society. But whatever the differences in form, the core of the injustice remains the same: in each case, an institutionalized pattern of cultural value constitutes some social actors as less than full members of society and prevents them from participating as peers. (Fraser 2000, p. n/p)

The notion of (mis)recognition might contribute to a reevaluation of the effects of legal and institutional translation by inquiring into the (un)even construction of the subjectivities involved in the intercultural encounter. In this regard, it helps to discover that, despite the dominant emphasis on *sameness* in this field – i.e., on the *accurate* and *precise* rendering of the message –, every legal and institutional translation is much more than an informational operation. Rather, it is also an act with deep identitarian implications, in which either the languages, cultures and groups involved might feel that their singularities and differences are recognized and, thus, through which a sense of belonging is developed, or through which feelings of distance and alienation may be triggered, perhaps by often inconspicuous mechanisms of subordination which might act in the marginalization and even the exclusion of the alleged target community. By shifting emphasis from "sameness" to the importance of incorporating the management of "differences" into the debates on equivalence, the notion of recognition helps to approach the relation between translation and justice in a different manner. In this regard, in an article which problematizes the correlation between material redistribution and cultural recognition, Pham (2013, p. abstract) also perceives that "the bridging itself must be sensitive to the different cultural frameworks [...] To fail to do this, the translator, despite her good will of bringing in justice, may do more harm than good." In our opinion, it might well be the case that, even if dominant translation models in legal and institutional settings live up to the expectations linked to redistribution, they might perhaps be still far away from meeting the requirements of recognition. In this regard, analyzing legal and institutional translation through the prism of (mis)recognition might expose the existence of "institutionalized patterns of subordination" at work in translation which, according to Fraser's theories (2002, p. 26), could prevent certain identities from fully participating in the co-construction of reality and social life on a par with other actors, a fact also alerted to by Fricker (2007) with her concept of "hermeneutical injustice," i.e. the difficulties faced by certain groups to make sense (which, for our purposes, may also mean to *convey* the sense) of their particular experiences. The following section will address a number of the factors which, in our day and age, might be aggravating translation's potential proclivity to exert symbolic violence in legal and institutional settings.

Institutionalized symbolic violence in dominant translation practices in legal and institutional settings

Current literature which has embraced the notion of recognition aims at challenging and reversing inequality-creating mechanisms which result in what Pierre Bourdieu has termed "symbolic violence" against certain identities and groups. One of the main features both of misrecognition and symbolic violence which has been stressed in reference works (Bourdieu 1998; Fraser 2000) is their structural character – i.e. their embeddedness in everyday practices, through which they are internalized as natural or inescapable, to the extent that they go either unquestioned or even unnoticed. Extrapolating these views on translation, and more precisely on legal and institutional translation, is enlightening, inasmuch as it helps to go beyond the detection of blunders, errors and pitfalls in the translation and intercultural transfer of ideologically-charged elements, enabling the discovery of the perverse and undesired effects of the very ideology of translation as a professional practice — i.e., of institutionalized ideas on translation underpinning the dominant norms regulating cross-cultural transfer.

In this regard, the prevailing expectation and common shaping of translation as an exact replica and of legal and institutional translators as impartial and non-intervening conduits, despite its powerful grip in legal and institutional contexts, can be considered to be an important cause resulting in misrecognition and symbolic violence in our global, multicultural, plural and diverse societies. If one accepts as a starting point that languages and cultures differ in their textual styles and traditions, in their rhetorical and argumentative patterns, and, at a deeper level, in the worldview informing their linguistic manifestations, it follows that the emphasis on reproduction and uniformity necessarily involves the overlooking or denial of the differences of certain identities. In this regard, as it was stressed in the previous section on multilingualisms, it is important to bear in mind that, contrary to what is proclaimed in dominant discourses, languages do not enjoy equal status in our day and age. To the contrary, they are vertically stratified and asymmetrically interrelated with other languages within a global order which some authors have defined as a "radial" system (Peña Martín 2005) –in which messages are forced to travel across the center in order to travel from one peripheral position to another different point in the periphery. The status of "procedural languages" conferred to German, French and English in the EU institutions, as well as the absolute predominance of English in the EU and other international organizations, are a clear manifestation of today's extremely hierarchical linguistic marketplace, and certainly raise doubts as regards the potential of minor languages and cultures to be heard in their own terms. In this line, certain authors who have inquired into the cross-cultural conceptual implications of so-called "global" discourses have questioned their universality and have leveled criticisms against the complicity of translation with neocolonial dynamics in the construction of transnationally shared meanings.

For instance, by observing the interpretation of the terminology related to human rights, Garre (1999) has concluded that formal uniformity does not guarantee common understanding and consistent appropriation of seemingly undisputed concepts such as "fair trial," "right to food" or "right to education." Adopting a cognitive approach, Garre suggests that translation should take as its starting point the acceptance of the contestedness and elusiveness of legal concepts and their inscription in particular cultural coordinates. Freeman (2013; [2002] 2017, p. 110) also notes that international human rights legislation is applied and construed differently at a local level. Rather than seeing translation merely as the cause of meaning distortion, Freeman also envisages translation as a solution. In this sense, in the line promoted by certain institutions, he advocates ways of translating and interpreting these rights which are respectful of cultural differences and which might be able to reconcile universality and diversity. Otherwise, as criticized by Mirza (2013) in the field of disability, the representation and verbalizations of disability in texts by international organizations run the risk of imposing the biased and reductive narratives and conceptualizations of dominant global powers. For Mirza, to the extent that these uniform discourses are shaped according to the views of the Northern hemisphere and are oblivious to the diverse cultural experiences of disability of non-hegemonic cultures, they paradoxically disable and exclude the communities for whom they are supposed to be speaking.

Certainly, in order to enable legal and institutional translation to be a site where differences might be taken into account and productively confronted, translators need to challenge the normative translation models inspired by the "ethics of sameness" so appreciated by institutions. They need to go beyond the strategies attuned to the translation behavior which, according to Mayoral (2003, p. 41-43), is dominant in official settings – a behavior which has been termed "translation by default" by Mayoral. This concept refers to the trend by which practitioners often opt for the most predictable, direct or automatic rendering, privileging literalist translation strategies even despite the conviction that, although it might not be the best translation option, it is certainly the safest technique given that it is the one expected by authorities. For the purposes of this article, it might be said that translation-by-default strategies might perhaps bring about translations which are "equivalent" and "adequate" from the point of view of redistribution, but, to play on words, might be considered to *default* on its duties if assessed from the perspective of recognition. In this sense, recognition imposes the extra task on translators of promoting the self-identification of the groups involved and the mutual intelligibility of differences.

Many are the authors who have criticized the alienating and/or misleading effects of translations which stick to the hegemonic "minimalist" translation model in legal and institutional settings. From their experience translating official documents from the minor languages of migrant communities in Spain, authors including Alkhalifa (1999), Mayoral (1995), Martin and Taibi (2010) and Taibi and Ozolins (2016) warn against the risks of literal translation strategies which, by reproducing the unfamiliar linguistic and textual patterns of certain cultures, might fuel intercultural suspicion and misunderstanding. In this regard, inasmuch as it further foreignizes individuals who are regarded as foreigners, this translation modality might take part in the construction of the Other as radically Other. Focusing specifically on the workings of translation in international organizations, authors including Koskinen (2000; 2008) and Biel (2014) have explored the causes of reactions of disapproval or estrangement aroused by institutional translation. By analyzing Finnish versions of legislation produced in the European Union, Koskinen perceives that, due to differences in textual and linguistic conventions, the authenticated Finnish versions are perceived as solemn, abstract and distant by their intended recipients, a readership used to a legal style which privileges readability and clarity. For our purposes, equivalence might meet the requirements of professional practice, but might be said to fall short of the goal of Law to achieve citizens' support to the social contract established within them. In a recent study on the features of EU texts translated into Polish, Biel (2014, p. 72-75) identifies initial feelings of rejection by recipients who were confronted with early-stage translations which blatantly challenged their expectancy norms. In this sense, Biel's work analyses the characteristics of the "textual fit" of original pre-accession Polish texts, of EU translated texts, and of post-accession original Polish texts. Her study suggests that the feelings of surrender and resignation generated by translations which showed a prevalence of literalness in the first stages gave way to the adoption of a Polish legal style which gradually incorporated and borrowed features from the dominant EU textual fit. Even when this can be considered to be a productive hybridization of the autochthonous conventions, the contribution of Polish in the reverse direction clearly reveals that translation practices are not only influenced by, but may also enhance, existing power differentials among languages, and even among language varieties.

In this regard, the conclusions of corpus-based studies on translation behavior are also pertinent. If general studies on "universals" have signaled a tendency of translation towards linguistic appropriateness, simplification and disambiguation (Mauranen and Kujamäki 2004, p. 1), authors who have studied legal and institutional translation have rather perceived strategies tending towards an institutionalization of the message and a burocratization of style, in turn resulting in a loss of metaphorical evocation (Koskinen 2008, p. 149) and in the neutralization of marked, value-laden vocabulary (Alcaraz Varó and Hughes 2002, p. 44). Whereas translation is often portrayed as the key to mutual understanding among cultures and individuals considered to be peers in abstract terms, the dominant ideology of translation could perhaps be curtailing the possibilities of translation to attain this goal. This tendency to accommodate translated texts to the prototypical entextualizations of the institution may in fact be the result of another structural factor exerting symbolic violence, namely, the centripetal force of the institutionalized varieties of major languages. The resulting translated texts may be perceived to be out of touch with standard language use by native language and second language users alike. The prevalence of *translationese* in authenticated language versions, due to the combination of literalist translation practices with centripetal forces within languages, might perhaps force us to nuance the optimism in Eco's oft-quoted statement that "translation is the language of Europe" and in institutional discourses on translation.

With a constructive purpose, introducing a diachronic perspective into the discussion might prove to be revealing. In fact, as has been warned by authors including Pierre Bourdieu (1998) and Nancy Fraser (2000), what makes domination and misrecognition more difficult to combat is their tendency to be perceived as natural and normal, as eternal and ahistorical, as inescapable. However, their transformation may be initiated by exposing the sociohistorical contingency of internalized power relations and of the normative practices legitimating and reproducing them. Legal and institutional translations are expected and often required to be bound to the seemingly indisputable principle of sameness, which is normativized in explicit operational rules such as the "verbatim interpretation requirement" at work in court interpreting (Mikkelson 1998), the "linguistic concordance" expected in the European Union which has already been mentioned (Strandvik 2002, p. 461) or the "semantic, formal and functional correspondence" demanded in the United Nations (Nóbrega 2010, p. 25). The search of "visual equivalence" and of "surface-level similarity," by selecting a "sameness format" and following the "full-stop rule" have been identified as compulsory, naturalized behavior by translators working at international organizations (Koskinen 2000, p. 55-56; Sosoni 2005, p. 85; Šarčević [1997] 2000, p. 117). However, the comparison of translations produced at different points in recent history demonstrates that the imperative nature of these constraints has become more stringent over a relatively short period of time.

The United Nations General Assembly in Paris proclaimed the Universal Declaration of Human Rights on December 1948. The English and Spanish versions of this text showed what could be called a "deceptive" but "empowering" symmetry:

Whereas <u>recognition of the inherent dignity and of the equal and inalienable rights of all members of the human family</u> is the foundation of freedom, justice and peace in the world,	Considerando que la libertad, la justicia y la paz en el mundo tienen por base el <u>reconocimiento de la dignidad intrínseca y de los derechos iguales e inalienables de todos los miembros de la familia humana</u>;
Whereas disregard and contempt for human rights have resulted in barbarous acts <u>which have outraged</u> the conscience of mankind, and *the advent of a world in which human beings shall enjoy **freedom of speech and belief and freedom from fear and want** has been* proclaimed <u>*as the highest aspiration of the common people*</u>, [...]	Considerando que el desconocimiento y el menosprecio de los derechos humanos han originado actos de barbarie <u>ultrajantes para</u> la conciencia de la humanidad, y que se ha proclamado, <u>*como la aspiración más elevada del hombre*</u>, *el advenimiento de un mundo en que los seres humanos,* **liberados del temor y de la miseria**, *disfruten de la* **libertad de palabra y de la libertad de creencias**; [...]
Article 1. All human beings are born free and equal in dignity and <u>rights. *They are endowed with reason and conscience **and*** </u> should act towards one another in a spirit of brotherhood.	Artículo 1 Todos los seres humanos nacen libres e iguales en dignidad y <u>derechos y, *dotados*</u> *como están de razón y conciencia*, deben comportarse fraternalmente los unos con los otros.

Despite its apparent visual equivalence, the room for maneuver tapped into by the Spanish translators vis-à-vis the English text – and also vis-à-vis the French text[2] – is considerable. The translation shifts in the clauses in the

---

[2] Considérant que la reconnaissance de la dignité inhérente à tous les membres de la famille humaine et de leurs droits égaux et inaliénables constitue le fondement de la liberté, de la justice et de la paix dans le monde.
Considérant que la méconnaissance et le mépris des droits de l'homme ont conduit à des actes de barbarie qui révoltent la conscience de l'humanité et que l'avènement d'un monde où les êtres humains seront libres de parler et de croire, libérés de la terreur et de la misère, a été proclamé comme la plus haute aspiration de l'homme. [...]
Article premier

preamble show a search for naturalness in language use. The translation shifts in the Spanish clauses in the preamble show a creative attitude, taking advantage of stylistic resources of Spanish legalese: strategic changes in the order of the items at sentence level both vis-à-vis the English and the French text, shifts in the grammatical categories used for the expression of different concepts (seen in the management of the different types of freedom referred to in this document, which at the same time respects the acceptability thresholds of each language), and a search for naturalness in language use are visible. Article 1 offers another example along the same lines: the Spanish text replaces coordination sentence-building devices by subordinate structures and transforms juxtaposition relations into coordination links, most probably to avoid the cultural perception of short sentences as blunt in legal Spanish.

In contrast with this subtle exploitation of the rhetoric and collocational patterns and usual features of each language, the English and Spanish version of two fragments from a Resolution published by the UN General Assembly in 2015, selected at random for the purposes of this study, show a move towards what could be called "total symmetry" in textual terms, achieved by the mimetic adherence to the English syntax by the Spanish text:

4. Urges all Member States requesting exemption under Article 19 of the Charter to submit as much information as possible in support of their requests and to consider submitting such information in advance of the deadline specified in resolution 54/237 C so as to enable the collation of any additional detailed information that may be necessary;	4. Insta a todos los Estados Miembros que soliciten la exención prevista en el Artículo 19 de la Carta a que presenten la mayor cantidad de información posible en apoyo de sus solicitudes y a que consideren la posibilidad de presentar esa información antes del plazo indicado en la resolución 54/237 C para permitir la reunión de cualquier información detallada adicional que pueda ser necesaria;

Tous les êtres humains naissent libres et égaux en dignité et en droits. Ils sont doués de raison et de conscience et doivent agir les uns envers les autres dans un esprit de fraternité.

5.	5.
Agrees that the failure of the Comoros, Guinea-Bissau, Sao Tome and Principe, Somalia and Yemen to pay the full minimum amount necessary to avoid the application of Article 19 of the Charter was due to conditions beyond their control; http://www.un.org/en/ga/search/view_doc.asp?symbol=A/RES/70/2	Conviene en que el hecho de que las Comoras, Guinea-Bissau, Santo Tomé y Príncipe, Somalia y el Yemen no hayan pagado íntegramente la cantidad mínima necesaria para evitar la aplicación del Artículo 19 de la Carta se debió a circunstancias ajenas a su voluntad; http://www.un.org/es/comun/docs/?symbol=A/RES/70/2

If the Spanish text can be said to be equivalent in terms of visual correspondence, it proves to be awkward and faulty when assessed as an independent text. The taken-for-granted ideal of mirroring the source text in the field of institutional translation offers a very different reading when judged merely from the point of view of a culture which clearly yields to the magnetic force of the language which today occupies the position of the source text and has turned into a trend-setting standard – a fact that the analysis of the French text confirms.[3] The degree of repetition and the strange word order used in Spanish acts against the text's readability. As shown by the telling example commented upon by Sosoni (2011) – a Danish sentence composed of 57 words between the subject and the corresponding verb –, the search for equality at a linguistic level makes translation flout its basic commitment to the expectation of intelligibility, let alone to stylistic elegance.

Given that the increased technologization of translation provision in general, and in international organizations in particular, has recently fostered a revival of literalism, the adoption of a recognition perspective may help us to wonder, in the line suggested by Koskinen (2008, p. 67), whether it is

---

[3] 4. Demande instamment à tous les États Membres qui demandent à bénéficier d'une dérogation à l'Article 19 de la Charte de fournir à l'appui de leur demande des renseignements aussi complets que possible et d'envisager de les communiquer avant l'expiration du délai fixé dans la résolution 54/237 C, afin de permettre le rassemblement de tous les renseignements détaillés complémentaires qui pourraient être requis ;

5. Convient que le non-paiement par les Comores, la Guinée-Bissau, le Libéria, la République centrafricaine, Sao Tomé-et-Principe, la Somalie et le Tadjikistan de la totalité du montant minimal requis pour éviter l'application de l'Article 19 de la Charte est dû à des circonstances indépendantes de leur volonté ;

https://documents-dds-ny.un.org/doc/UNDOC/GEN/N07/463/84/PDF/N0746384.pdf?OpenElement

possible for translators to resist mechanical models of translation further enhanced by an increasingly machine-aided translation process. Certainly, although this reflection is not intended to question the virtues in terms of efficiency of translation tools which, in any event, are here to stay, it may perhaps be useful for the purpose of raising awareness about the ideologized implications accompanying recent developments in the profession, and ultimately for the purpose of developing counterstrategies which may mitigate the pernicious effects of these recent, yet already structural factors in current translation practice generating institutional violence. For, even in the increasingly automated contexts in the legal and institutional realm, other translation models are possible; other regimes for the expression and recognition of differences can be created.

Creative imagination at the service of recognition in and through translation

The concept of recognition serves as a solid foundation for the critique of existing power relations and of the subtle mechanisms legitimizing and reproducing them, also including translation practices themselves. This critique, in turn, may also be a useful stepping stone to alternative translation practices. Certainly, if recognition is considered to have a dialogical and contextual nature, no strategy can be regarded or proclaimed as a panacea *ad infinitum*. Furthermore, a strategy which may be effective from the point of view of recognition in one context may have the reverse impact in a different setting. For this reason, creative imagination necessarily needs to be an ally of translators in the pursuit of a moving target such as recognition.

Nevertheless, and without any intention of reifying them or of being prescriptive, some existing examples can be inspirational for the rethinking and rebranding of today's dominant practices. At an abstract level, Koskinen (2008) calls for legal and institutional translation to be approached as a "reflexive practice." In this regard, translation professionals need to develop an awareness of the role that institutional translation plays in the shaping of societies and in the negotiation of identities, in general, and of the side-effects which may potentially be brought about by the acritical imposition of sameness on diverse societies. Koskinen's (2010) proposal to search both for "effective" and "affective" communication strategies may serve as an additional guideline for practitioners in order for them to approach texts and languages not merely as instances of communication, but as sites for identification and discovery both of the Self and of the Other. This awareness may serve as a springboard for translated products which do not hesitate to challenge and resist the seemingly indisputable requirement of identicalness with a view to cater for the expectations of the readership or for the user's needs in order to enable them to adequately manage the Other's specificities.

At a theoretical and methodological level, certain translation scholars have taken into account those reflections on the issue of linguistic relativity expressed by authors including Humboldt, Sapir and Whorf, Wierzbicka, etc., who maintain that language(s) influence(s) thought and meaning to varying degrees. In this regard, Juliane House (2000) relativizes non-translatability, but also argues for a more pragmatic model of translation and translation criticisms; one which incorporates a cultural filter in order to address linguacultural differences responsibly and dynamically, depending on the nature of the commission. At a more practical level, and merely by way of illustration, the courage to overstep professional norms to address the unprecedented challenges of difference can be considered to be epitomized at a conceptual level in the explanatory techniques which are argued for in the field of Public Service Interpreting and Translation in order to warn about cultural gaps instead of merely erasing them or bridging them unproblematically for the participants (Bischoff et al. 2009, p. 18-19). It can also be perceived to be realized at a textual level in the "creative" Canadian translations analyzed by Šarčević (2010; [1997] 2000), which, subsequent to the institutional declaration that "literal translation violates the principle of equal language rights" (Šarčevič [1997] 2000, p. 47), have been produced for several decades in co-drafting processes in which the linguistic and textual features of both French and English are respected in "equivalent" versions which, nevertheless, differ to a great extent in their visual appearance:

I, ... do solemnly swear that I will faithfully, truly and to the best of my judgment, skill and ability, execute and perform the duties required of me as director (officer or employee as the case may be) of the Canada Mortgage and Housing Corporation and which properly relate to any office or position in the Corporation held by me.	Je, ..., jure de bien et fidèlement remplir les fonctions, attachées à l'emploi (ou au poste) que j'occupe à la Société canadienne d'hypothèques et de logement.
Where a notice, advertisement or other matter is printed in one or more publications pursuant to section (1), it shall be given equal prominence in each official language.	Il est donné dans ces textes égale importance aux deux langues officielles.

No husband is compellable to disclose any communication made to him by his wife during their marriage, and no wife is compellable to disclose any communication made to her by her husband during their marriage.	Nul ne peut être contraint de divulguer une communication que son conjoint lui a faite durant leur mariage. (Šarčevič [1997] 2000, p. 184, 187)

The same courage may also be considered to be embodied at both terminological and language level in the intervenient translations of health-related texts made by the social change project Soul City in South Africa. As explained by Kruger (2010), in order to ensure accessibility and acceptability by a wide readership not necessarily familiar with or tolerant of Western discourses and terms related to the prevention of sexually transmitted diseases, translators find culturally-sensitive ways to make prevention messages accessible with direct language which, nevertheless, avoids being offensive. For this purpose, as against the usual trend for translations to cling to the institutionalized, "major" language and language variety, the employment of non-standard uses and of explanatory techniques is encouraged in the translation brief: "[u]se *simple* vocabulary: more *common* synonyms, not necessarily 'pure' language, loan words and indigenized loan words are allowed. Also, if you use an English loan word, please *add* the meaning of the English loan word in your language."

Obviously, the possibilities for articulating recognition in translation are neither limited to nor exhausted in the above examples. By definition, recognition is in its very nature utopian and ultimately unrealizable. Observing that recognition claims are highly indeterminate, Kompridis (2007, p. 287) suggests that "[p]erhaps we need to work towards practices of recognition that do not already have form or place in our social life, expressive practices which are nonetheless continuous with self-criticism, engaging the misrecognized and misrecognizers in ways we can't yet describe". Legal and institutional translation faces acute, yet fascinating challenges. As Richard Sennett states in *Respect in a World of Inequality*, "the acts which convey respect –the act of acknowledging others– are demanding and obscure" (Sennett 2011, p. 59). Any future legal or institutional translation might be an occasion not to merely follow norms, but also to resist and challenge their limitations in order to voice the experience of the identities involved in an ever more respectful manner. Any future legal or institutional translation presents us with an opportunity to attempt to imaginatively live up to the enthralling demands of recognition.

Funding

This article is a result of a research project entitled VIOSIMTRAD ("Symbolic Violence and Translation: Challenges in the Representation of Fragmented Identities within the Global Society", FFI2015-66516- P; MINECO/FEDER, EU), carried out by the Research group TRADIC (Traducción, Ideología, Cultura) at University of Salamanca and financed by the Spanish Ministerio de Economía y Competitividad and FEDER funds.

References

Alcaraz Varó, Enrique & Brian Hughes, 2002. *Legal Translation Explained.* Manchester: St. Jerome.

Alkhalifa, Waleed Saleh, 1999. El tortuoso camino de la traducción: la traducción jurídica del árabe. *In:* Miguel Hernando De Larramendi, Juan Pablo Arias & Mohamed Arkoun, eds. *Traducción, emigración y culturas.* Cuenca: Universidad de Castilla-La Mancha, 231-240.

Ayuso, Silvia, 2017. La Casa Blanca de Donald Trump elimina el español de su página 'web', *El País,* Madrid. Online: http://internacional.elpais.com/internacional/2017/01/22/estados_unidos/1485105920_597756.html.

Bassnett, Susan & André Lefevere, eds., 1998. *Constructing Cultures: Essays on Literary Translation,* Clevedon: Multilingual Matters.

Biel, Łucja, 2014. *Lost in the Eurofog. The Textual Fit of Translated Law.* Frankfurt am Main: Peter Lang.

Bischoff, Alexander, Louis Loutan & Sofía García Beyaert, 2009. *En otras palabras. Guía para la consulta médica intercultural.* Geneva: Universal Doctor Project.

Blommaert, Jan, 2013. *Ethnography, Superdiversity and Linguistic Landscapes: Chronicles of Complexity.* Bristol: Multilingual Matters.

Blommaert, Jan & Ben Rampton, 2011. Language and Superdiversity. *Diversities,* 13(2), 1-21.

Bourdieu, Pierre, 1998. *La domination masculine.* Paris: Seuil.

Castro, Olga, Sergi Mainer & Svetlana Page, 2017. Introduction: Self-Translation, from Minorisation to Empowerment. *In:* Olga Castro, Sergi Mainer & Svetlana Page, eds. *Self-Translation and Power. Negotiating Identities in European Multilingual Contexts.* London: Palgrave Macmillan, 1-22.

Couzens, Gerard, 2017. Spanish language content REMOVED from White House website after Trump inauguration, *Sunday Express,* London. Online: http://www.express.co.uk/news/world/757904/Spanish-language-White-House-website-Donald-Trump.

Craith, Máiréad Nic, 2006. *Europe and the Politics of Language.* Hampshire: Palgrave Macmillan.

Cronin, Michael, 1995. Altered States: Translation and Minority Languages. *TTR: Traduction, terminologie, rédaction,* 8(1), 85-103.

———, 2006. *Translation and Identity*. London: Routledge.
Dicker, Susan J., 1996. *Languages in America. A Pluralist View*. Clevedon, Philadelphia: Multilingual Matters.
Fraser, Nancy, 2000. Rethinking Recognition. *New Left Review*, 3, 107-120.
———, 2002. Recognition without Ethics. *In:* Scott Lash & Mike Featherstone, eds. *Recognition and Difference: Politics, Identity, Multiculture*. London: Sage, 20-42.
Fraser, Nancy & Axel Honneth, 2003. *Redistribution or Recognition: A Political-Philosophical Exchange*. translated by Joel Golb, James Ingram & Christianne Wilke. London: Verso.
Freeman, Michael, 2013. Universalism of Human Rights and Cultural Relativism. *In:* Scott Sheeran & Nigel Rodley, eds. *Routledge Handbook of International Human Rights Law*. London, New York: Routledge, 49-61.
———, [2002] 2017. *Human Rights: An Interdisciplinary Approach*. London: Polity Press.
Fricker, Miranda, 2007. *Epistemic Injustice. Power and the Ethics of Knowing*. Oxford: Oxford University Press.
Garre, Marianne, 1999. *Human Rights in Translation. Legal concepts in different languages*. Köpenhamn: Copenhagen Business School Press.
Hermans, Theo, 1999. *Translation in Systems. Descriptive and Systemic Approaches Explained*. Brooklands: St. Jerome.
Honneth, Axel, 1995. *The Struggle for Recognition. The Moral Grammar of Social Conflict*. translated by Joel Anderson. Cambridge: Polity Press.
House, Juliane, Rosario Martín Ruano & Nicole Baumgarten, eds., 2005. *Translation and the Construction of Identity*, Seoul: IATIS.
Karpinski, Eva C., 2015. Invisible Borders: Translation and Multilingualism in an Unequal World. *Tusaaji: A Translation Review* 3(3), 21-34.
Kompridis, Nikolas, 2007. Struggling over the Meaning of Recognition: A Matter of Identity, Justice, or Freedom? *European Journal of Political Theory*, 6(3), 277-289.
Koskinen, Kaisa, 2000. Institutional Illusions. Translating in the EU Commission. *The Translator*, 6(1), 49-65.
———, 2008. *Translating Institutions: an ethnographic study of EU translation*. Manchester: St. Jerome.
———, 2010. On EU Communication 2.0: Using Social Media to Attain Affective Citizenship. *In:* Mona Baker, Maeve Olohan & María Calzada Pérez, eds. *Text and Context*. Manchester: St. Jerome, 139-156.
Kruger, Alet, 2010. Translating Public Information Texts on Health Issues into Languages of Limited Diffusion in South Africa. *In:* Roberto Valdeón, ed. *Translating Information*. Eduino: Universidad de Oviedo, 150-166.
Lambert, José, 2013. La sociologie, l'interdisciplinarité et les recherches sur la traduction. *TTR: etudes sur le texte et ses transformations*, 262, 245-268.
Lantto, Hanna, 2016. A Tale of a City and Its Two Languages: A History of Bilingual Practices In the City Of Bilbao. *In:* Reetta Toivanen & Janne Saarikivi, eds. *Linguistic genocide or superdiversity? New and Old Language Diversities*. Bristol, Buffalo, Toronto: Multilingual Matters, 135-158.

Lash, Scott & Mike Featherstone, 2002. Recognition and Difference. *In:* Scott Lash & Mike Featherstone, eds. *Recognition and Difference: Politics, Identity, Multiculture.* London: Sage, 1-19.

Martin, Anne & Mustapha Taibi, 2010. Translating and Interpreting for the Police in Politicised Contexts: The case of Tayseer Allouny. *In:* Julie Boéri & Carol Maier, eds. *Compromiso Social y Traducción/Interpretación.* Granada: ECOS, 38-40, 214-226.

Mauranen, Anna & Pekka Kujamäki, 2004. Introduction. *In:* Anna Mauranen & Pekka KujamäKi, eds. *Translation Universals Do They Exist?* Amsterdam, Philadelphia: John Benjamins, 1-14.

Mayoral Asensio, Roberto, 1995. La traducción jurada del inglés al español de documentos paquistaníes: un caso de traducción reintercultural. *Sendebar,* 6, 115-146.

——, 2003. *Translating Official Documents.* New York: Routledge.

Meylaerts, Reine, 2011. Translational Justice in a Multilingual World: An Overview of Translational Regimes. *Meta: Journal des traducteurs,* 56(4), 743-757.

Mikkelson, Holly, 1998. Verbatim Interpretation: An Oxymoron. Online: http://www.acebo.com/pages/verbatim-interpretation-an-oxymoron.

Mirza, Mansha, 2013. Disability and Cross-border Mobility: comparing resettlement experiences of Cambodian and Somali refugees with disabilities. *In:* Michele Moore, ed. *Moving Beyond Boundaries Disability Studies.* London, New York: Routledge, 4-17.

Monzó Nebot, Esther, 2017. The Out-Grouping Society: Phrasemes Othering Minorities in the International Bill of Human Rights (English-French-Spanish). *In:* Stanislaw Goźdź-Roszkowski & Gianluca Pontrandolfo, eds. *Phraseology in Legal and Institutional Settings. A Corpus-based Interdisciplinary Perspective.* London: Routledge, 131-159.

Moreno Cabrera, Juan Carlos, 2016. *Multilingüismo y lenguas en contacto.* Madrid: Síntesis.

Niranjana, Tejaswini, 1992. *Siting Translation: History, Post-Structuralism, and the Colonial Context.* Berkeley: University of California Press.

Nóbrega, María, 2010. Presencia del español en las organizaciones internacionales: las Naciones Unidas. *Puntoycoma,* 117, 24-27. Online: http://ec.europa.eu/translation/bulletins/puntoycoma/117/pyc11710_es.htm.

O'Keefe, Ed, 2017. Looking for a Spanish version of WhiteHouse.gov? No existe — todavia, *The Washington Post,* Washington. Online: https://www.washingtonpost.com/news/powerpost/wp/2017/01/23/looking-for-a-spanish-version-of-whitehouse-gov-ya-no-existe/?utm_term=.8af73b13e4b2.

Peña Martín, Salvador, 2005. En pocas palabras (VI), *El Trujamán,* Madrid: Centro Virtual Cervantes. Online: http://cvc.cervantes.es/trujaman/anteriores/junio_05/10062005.htm.

Pham, Loc, 2013. Justice in Translation: From the Material to the Cultural. *Translation: a transdisciplinary Journal,* 2, 33-52.

Rosello, Mireille, 2012. Plurilingual Europeans in a Multilingual Europe: Incomplete and Imperfect Communication Tactics. *In:* Lszl Marácz & Mireille Rosello, eds. *Multilingual Europe, Multilingual European.* Amsterdam, New York: Rodopi, 215-233.

Šarčevič, Susan, 2010. Legal Translation in Multilingual Settings. *In:* Icíar Alonso, Jesús Baigorri & Helen Campbell, eds. *Translating Justice.* Granada: Comares, 19-45.

———, 2015. Language and Culture in EU Law: Introduction and Overview. *Language and Culture in EU Law: Multidisciplinary Perspectives.* London: Routledge, 1-14.

———, [1997] 2000. *New Approach to Legal Translation.* The Hague: Kluwer Law International.

Sennett, Richard, 2011. *Respect in a World of Inequality.* New York, London: Norton.

Sosoni, Vilelmini, 2005. Multilingualism in Europe. Blessing or curse? *In:* Albert Branchadell & Lovell Margaret West, eds. *Less Translated Languages.* Amsterdam: John Benjamins.

———, 2011. Training Translators to Work for the EU Institutions: Luxury or Necessity? *JoSTRans: The Journal of Specialised Translation,* 16, 77-108.

Strandvik, Ingemar, 2002. Transparencia, gobernanza y traducción: ¿ha llegado la hora de un enfoque funcional? *In:* Pollux Hernúñez & Luis González, eds. *Español, lengua de traducción. Actas del I Congreso Internacional.* Almagro: European Commission, EFE.

Taibi, Mustapha & Uldis Ozolins, 2016. *Community Translation.* New York: Bloomsbury Academic.

Taylor, Charles, 1994. The Politics of Recognition. *In:* Amy Gutmann, ed. *Multiculturalism. Examining the Politics of Recognition.* Princeton: Princeton University Press, 25-73.

Venuti, Lawrence, 1998a. Introduction. *The Translator,* 4(2), 135-144.

———, 1998b. *The Scandals of Translation. Towards an ethics of difference.* London: Routledge.

Vertovec, Steven, 2007. Super-diversity and its Implications. *Ethnic and Racial Studies,* 30(6), 1024-1054.

———, 2015. Introduction: Migration, cities, diversities 'old' and 'new'. *In:* Steven Vertovec, ed. *Diversities Old and New. Migration and Socio-Spatial Patterns in New York, Singapore and Johannesburg.* London: Palgrave Macmillan, 1-20.

Wagner, Emma, Svend Bech & Jesús M Martínez, 2002. *Translating for the European Union Institutions.* Manchester, Northampton: St. Jerome.

Chapter 4

Translating and interpreting cultures. Discussing translation and interpreting ethics in a postmonolingual age

Gernot Hebenstreit

Although the topic of translation/interpreting ethics has always been present in translation/interpreting studies, recent times have witnessed a rising interest in ethical issues. While many of the studies focus on moral issues impacting individual cases, there still is a lack of work on a conceptual and theoretical level. The aim of this paper is to contribute to discussions that may eventually lead to the establishment of translation ethics as a theoretical framework for researching moral and ethical issues of translation and interpreting. To this end, I will present the concept *translation culture* (*Translationskultur*) as defined by the Austrian translation studies scholar Erich Prunč (1997; 2000a; 2008) that has repeatedly been applied in the context of research on translation history and translation policy, and discuss its potential as well as its implications for ethical reasoning in translation/interpreting studies.

Introduction

In contrast to the widespread beliefs among consumers of translation/interpreting products and services on translation/interpreting being a mere act of copying source language material and pasting it in a target language text, in Translation and Interpreting Studies, the delusional nature of a translation's (an interpretation's, a translator's, or an interpreter's) neutrality has become a common *topos* over the years (cf. statements pointing out that translation does not take place in a *vacuum*). As theoretically oriented models increasingly portray translators/interpreters as powerful actors, as key players in fields of ideologies and politics, the ethical dimension of translation and interpreting becomes more evident. In the latest edition of his monograph on the tracks of translation studies, which may be said to enjoy canonical status in German-speaking translation/interpreting academia (see Schreiber 2011), the Austrian scholar Erich Prunč devotes a full chapter to translation ethics, in which he draws on earlier work in this field. This article seeks to discuss Prunč's conceptualization of translation ethics in order to make this scholar's ideas available to a greater audience and to further discussions on translation and interpreting ethics.

The need for an ethical stance

As Prunč points out (2012, p. 338), the topicality of translation ethics is strongly related to the role that translation plays in society. Recognized or not, translation and interpreting play a paramount role in the world we live in. Whether in visible or invisible forms, translation in today's globalized world has become an omnipresent institution of transcultural mediation, inherently transforming and filtering information, ideas, convictions, and values. Global phenomena like migration, the increasing geographical, occupational, social and other mobilities of the individual, together with processes of digitization contribute to the increasing permeability of what once might have been conceived of as clear-cut cultural borders. It is not so easy anymore to distinguish different cultural spaces. Our context is an overlap of fuzzy-edged spaces, hybrid forms of poly-cultural aggregation.

Against this background, it is safe to state that, even regions with no official history of language policies, have seen the dawn of a postmonolingual age. In such contexts, the selection of texts and their various rewritings deserve our utmost attention, even more so given the volatility of information in the age of the Internet. The developments in translation technology have already started to take away one-dimensional routine tasks from the translators' work plate and will continue to do so. What will stay on the human translators' work agenda is what Prunč calls "Bereich des kreativen und ethisch verantworteten Umganges mit Texten," i.e. textual work that demands creativity and ethical accountability (Prunč 2012, p. 337).

In the case of interpreting, it is even more obvious that interpreters may become part of a power game in the "Konstruktion von sozialem Sinn," that is, the construction of social sense (Prunč 2012, p. 237). Prunč challenges the legitimacy of positions that uphold concepts like 'distance' and 'objectivity' as main characteristics of 'professionalism' in the light of the insights into discursive processes being power-driven matters. He, therefore, calls for negotiations between the potentially involved action partners[1] about the

---

[1] The concept of 'action partner' largely draws on Holz-Mänttäri's (1984) conceptualization of translation as a complex action in which the translator cooperates with other experts fulfilling various roles in the production of a translation.

responsibilities interpreters are capable and willing to take in the design and management of communicative situations and in the discursive construction of social processes.

While the points mentioned so far may be regarded as external factors beckoning the need for an ethical foundation of translation and interpreting practice, it is interesting to reflect on how the overall development of translation and interpreting studies has been making room for the discussion of ethical aspects of translation and interpreting. Looking back at the past decades, an ongoing strife towards objects of research that lie more and more beyond the boundaries of "texts" (in a narrow understanding) becomes obvious. Instead of studying primarily the relations between signs and texts, researchers have moved their attention to functions, systems, cultures, agents.[2] The various turns in translation and interpreting studies gave birth to research on aspects like ideology, politics, power, gatekeeping, agency, and activism, all of which are in some way connected to choices taken in the course of human interaction (Hebenstreit 2017, p. 5). What goes hand in hand with this development is that, paraphrasing Prunč (2012, p. 338), the rigid binary distinction of *right* and *wrong* that may be found in conceptualizations of translation within the earlier normative and equivalence-based models gave way to thinking in terms of continua of possible solutions that take into account specific contexts and situations. Last but not least, postmodern thinking, namely deconstruction, see translators and interpreters in a role radically opposite to that of invisible transcoders. Translators and interpreters now appear as visible co-creators of intellectual spaces, textual worlds, and cultures. Prunč sees as a major task for translation ethics to explore the boundaries of the thus created spaces of freedom (Prunč 2012, p. 338).

Indeed, reflecting about translation and interpreting ethics presuppose that we ascribe roles to translators and interpreters which involve responsibility for decisions taken in the process of translating and interpreting. In order to be able to make decisions, there must be freedom of choice. If there is no such freedom, it is not possible to indulge in ethical discussions, as the assumption of freedom is situated at the very core of ethics (see Schweppenhäuser 2003; Pieper 2007).

Translation/interpreting culture

Erich Prunč introduced the concept of *Translationskultur* in an article in 1997 and continued to elaborate on the concept in the coming years (see especially

---

[2] For a discussion of translation and interpreting studies as a study of relations see Chesterman (2004).

Prunč 2000a; 2000b; 2001; 2008). Since the German term 'Translation' designates a concept that is superordinate to the concepts *translation* and *interpreting*, it seems advisable to use 'translation and interpreting culture' or 'translation/interpreting culture' in English. This provides the possibility to distinguish between *translation cultures* and *interpreting cultures*, where necessary. Prunč defines *translation/interpreting culture* as follows:

> "Unter Translationskultur ist das historisch gewachsene, sich aus der dialektischen Beziehung zur Translationspraxis entwickelnde, selbstreferentielle und selbstregulierende Subsystem einer Kultur zu verstehen, das sich auf das Handlungsfeld Translation bezieht. Sie besteht aus einem Set von gesellschaftlich etablierten, gesteuerten und steuerbaren Normen, Konventionen, Erwartungshaltungen, Wertvorstellungen und habitualisierten Verhaltensmustern aller in der jeweiligen Kultur aktuell oder potentiell an Translationsprozessen beteiligten Handlungspartner."[3] (Prunč 2012, p. 340)

Thus, *translation/interpreting culture* is a subsystem of a culture relating to the action field (cf. below) of translation. This cultural subsystem is historically grown and constantly developing in a dialectical relation to the practice that is being performed in the field. It is made up of a set of socially established norms, conventions, expectations, ideals, and habitualized patterns of behavior shared by all action partners that are actually or potentially involved in the given culture. They are all seen as being both steered and steerable. Prunč sees *translation culture* as a social construct that is embedded in a culture and that reflects social consensus and dissent about allowed, recommended, and obligatory forms of translation and interpreting. Being a social construct, it is the result of a balance of interests of individuals and institutions that are engaged in the various autonomous and heteronomous fields of translation and interpreting (Prunč 2012, p. 340). In ethical terms, Prunč (2000a) conceives *translation/interpreting culture* as a deontic system. Looking back, this was not always explicit. Indeed, in the 1997 formulation of the concept, its ethical dimension was not yet clear.

---

[3] "Translation/Interpreting culture is the historically developed, self-referential and self-regulating sub-system of a culture that relates to the field of translation, which derives from a dialectical relationship to translation practice. It consists of a set of socially established, controlled and controllable norms, conventions, expectations, value propositions and naturalized behavioral patterns shared by all actors actually or potentially involved in the translation processes within the relevant culture" (editor's translation).

In my understanding, the birth of translation/interpreting culture was the result of the author's efforts in advancing functionalist thinking on translation. Being a functionalist with a deep interest in and broad understanding of systemic approaches to translation and interpreting based on cultural studies, Prunč was well aware of the blind spots in the functionalist conceptualization of translation and interpreting, namely the action-theory-based models of Vermeer (Reiß and Vermeer 1984) and Holz-Mänttäri (1984). The main issue at stake here is the implied equality of the involved players; i.e. equality in terms of possibilities to realize one's goals in given settings. One way to overcome the constricted vision represented in these models was to embed functionalist thinking in a framework that would take into account broader social contexts, integrate a broader understanding of culture, and take power, status and agenda into consideration.

In the following years, Prunč devotes some effort to identifying elements of translation/interpreting cultures, i.e. issues that can become the object of norms, conventions, expectations, ideals and habitualized patterns of behavior. He does so not by creating some sort of systematic inventory, but rather by integrating a number of research questions in his work. The identification of relevant elements is partly the result of his interpretation of empirical data, partly the result of theoretical reflections. Among the elements identified, we find: parameters of quality (1997; 2000a), loyalties (1997; 2002), directionality (2000a), role of mother tongue and foreign language acquisition (2000a), institutionalized translation/interpreting training (2000a), fields of translation/interpreting (2000a; 2005d); standard relations between source text and target text (2000a; 2001; 2002; 2005d), conventional *skopoi* (1997; 2002), status of translation/interpreting (2001; 2005d), roles and visibility of translators/interpreters (2005d), selection of source texts (2005a). The author (2005c; 2005b; 2008) then integrates sociological thinking into his reasoning by embracing Bourdieu's conceptualization of field,[4] capital, and habitus.

Prunč's translation/interpreting culture has been well received by some scholars working on historical topics (see Schippel 2008; Syrjänen 2014) who most probably were intrigued by this framework's ability to integrate various translation/interpreting studies approaches. These scholars were thus answering Prunč's call (1997; 2012) that the description of translation/interpreting cultures should be a major task for translation and interpreting studies. This call has a descriptive core, but it is Prunč's

---

[4] Especially in his 2008 paper, Prunč's translation/interpreting culture seems very close to Bourdieu's *field*. For a critical comparison of these two concepts, see Wolf (2010).

conviction that translation and interpreting studies should get actively involved in the shaping of translation/interpreting culture, and further one that is organized democratically, where translators and interpreters, as equals among others, can act as the afore-mentioned co-creators of intellectual spaces, textual worlds, and cultures (Prunč 2012, p. 339). One might argue that, on the level of theoretical modeling, Prunč rejects the implied assumption of total equality of action partners underlying Holz-Mänttäri's thinking, but personally shares this author's values. One step towards what today might still be deemed a "utopia" (Prunč 2012, p. 342) would be the improvement of the social status of translation/interpreting and translators/interpreters, demanding a joint effort by individuals, professional organizations, and academia. This call, voiced in 1997, still stands valid today.

It is in his 2008 article where Prunč most explicitly voices this call by reflecting on the principles underlying the construction of a democratic translation/interpreting culture: *cooperativeness* (Kooperativität), *loyalty* (Loyalität), *transparency* (Transparenz), and *ecologicality* (Ökologizität). From a terminological point of view, all these principles appear as categories, types of characteristics that can be used to distinguish between different types of translation/interpreting cultures. When looking at a particular culture under the glass of *cooperativeness*, 'lack of cooperation,' 'reluctance towards cooperation,' 'intense cooperation,' 'strong preference for cooperation,' and so forth may be applicable and all reflect some degree of 'cooperativeness.' Such a continuum can also be found in the other principles. The German suffixes '-ivität' in 'Kooperativität,' and '-izität' in 'Ökologizität,' respectively, express both the state of being something and the scalability of that something. If these categories are to serve as guiding principles, it is implicitly understood that to further a democratic translation/interpreting culture means to strive for conditions that maximize scores under the cooperation, loyalty, transparency and ecology continua.

In Prunč's *cooperation* a respect for the legitimate interests of all action partners is implied, the willingness to negotiate sound solutions, e.g. in the form of conventions, to balance these interests and the lasting reduction and prevention of conflicts is also an important aspect in terms of a translation/interpreting culture's *ecology* (Prunč 2008, p. 30). As for *loyalty*, an important property is that it is not a one-way street, binding only the translator/interpreter to the source-text author, the commissioner of the translation, and/or the recipient in the target culture. Prunč strongly rejects any kind of unidirectionalism in seeing loyalty as a multilateral principle that connects and binds all action partners. He rightly points out that there is also a loyalty towards the translators/interpreters professional community, and – last but not least – there is a loyalty towards herself/himself (2008, p. 31).

When translation/interpreting takes place in situations of irresolvable conflict of interests, the translator/interpreter has to take responsibility for acting to the (dis)advantage of action partners. *Transparency* is essential in creating mutual trust among the action partners and the translator/interpreter. It involves the clarification of the *skopos* and the conditions, the verification of translation/interpreting and backtracking of decisions, but also aspects like authorship and responsibilities (2008, p. 32). Finally, the *ecology* principle aims at preserving resources in the widest sense of the word. It's not only about efficiency, but also about sustainability, i.e. taking into account long-term consequences at the social and cultural levels in the participating cultures, including the translation/interpreting culture.

Translation/interpreting culture and translation ethics

While the ethical dimension was always implicit in Prunč's writings, particularly embedded in translator's responsibilities, questions of loyalty, and types of translation (Prunč sees the refusal and the decline of translation/interpreting as types of translatorial action), it is the constructive principles of cooperation, loyalty, transparency and ecology that connect *translation/interpreting culture* to translation ethics. From an ethical perspective, these principles may be interpreted as moral virtues that serve moral *values*. Value theory and virtue ethics constitute two of many approaches within ethics (understood here as a branch of philosophy) that, in my opinion, fit well with a large part of the ethical discourse in translation/interpreting studies (see Hebenstreit 2010).[5]

Value theory suggests that in evaluating actions from a moral stance, values are to be taken as the measure. Moral values comprise a community's shared beliefs about what is good and what is better, as these values are structured in hierarchies. Moral judgment gives an answer to the question 'to what degree these values have been upheld by a particular action.' The particular choice of values and their concrete definitions may differ from group to group, thus value systems are culture specific. Prunč draws on Pieper (2007) who argues that a western, democratically structured culture would display a hierarchy of values like this one:

---

[5] This decision does of course not imply any kind of superiority of virtue ethics and value theory over other ethical theories or approaches like consequentialism, or deontology in the discussion of translation/interpreting ethics. I am interested in the ways of ethical reasoning in translation and interpreting studies, and in my estimation Prunč's model lends itself towards values-and-virtues-based reasoning, as do many discussions on professional codes of ethics.

The top level of the hierarchy is occupied by *basic ethical values*[6] that are deeply anchored in the concept of human dignity: freedom (e.g. freedom of the person, freedom of religion, freedom of conscience, freedom of expression, freedom of scientific research, freedom of artistic expression) and justice (e.g. equality).

On the second level, we find *moral values* that guide the members of the action group to lead a good life. Among these values we find:

- personal values (e.g. self-determination, self-responsibility, love, friendship, quality of life, health);

- social values (e.g. solidarity, fairness, collective responsibility); and

- ecological values (e.g. sustainability).

The third level holds *economic values* (e.g. free economy, freedom of contract, profitability, added value, property, goods, money).

Such value hierarchies play an important role in finding decisions in situations of moral dilemma, in private, political and professional milieus. The moral values relevant to our discussion, those of a professional community, would be located on the second and third level of this hierarchy. For the translation profession, Chesterman has identified the following values (1997, p. 150-156): *clarity, truth, trust,* and *understanding. Clarity* is a value related to the message, which is produced by the translator and needs to be understood by its addressees. *Truth* is a value realized by the relation between source text and target text. *Trust*, on the other hand, is an interpersonal value essential for successful communication. It might not be obvious at first glance why *understanding* should qualify as a value. When discussing *understanding*, Chesterman draws on Christian theology, where *understanding* can be read as a metaphor for love that involves the caring about others and the responsibility to prevent others from harm. In the case of translation to uphold the value of *understanding* means preventing the communication partners from "communicative suffering" (1997, p. 156).

In his commitment to a democratic translation/interpreting culture, Prunč lists *human rights, human dignity, tolerance, respect for the otherness of others, equality of opportunities* (with reference to Cronin 1998), *solidarity, openness to dialogue and consensus, emancipation of deprived and of minorities* (with reference to Venuti 1998), *economical use of resources, minimization of conflicts,* and *sustainability* as top level values

---

[6] Here it is 'ethical' because *freedom* and *justice* form two concepts at the very center of ethical reasoning.

(Prunč 2012, p. 358). Contrasting these values with Chesterman's *clarity, truth, trust,* and *understanding,* there are striking differences not only in terms of numbers. The values assembled by Chesterman are conceptually and linguistically in line with the tradition of classical ethics, partly going back to ancient Greek philosophy. The values, as complicated as they may prove in relation to real-life moral problems, appear as simple, in the sense of basic, elementary, self-contained, entities. The values in Prunč's list appear to be of a more complex nature at a conceptual level and evoke associations with ethical, or maybe even political discourse on topical issues of globalization. Before looking any further into the differences, let us have a look at the virtues involved.

Values are closely related to virtues because, in order to achieve certain values in the course of an action within the framework of virtue ethics, it is necessary that the action is grounded in the actor's virtues. The moral evaluation of an action aims not at the action itself, but at the actor's 'character,' if you will, taking a comprehensive account of his or her ways of moral reasoning, feeling and acting. Virtues need to be appropriated by practice and imitation (not by the study of moral principles) (Nida-Rümelin 2005, p. 36). Prunč speaks of 'principles,' not virtues; it is, however, my understanding that, in the course of constructing a democratic translation/interpreting culture, these principles act as virtues. In virtue ethics, virtues have always been seen as a means to achieve some greater goal like the 'Kingdom of God' in Christian virtue ethics or, in a more general manner, the 'good life.' The perception of this 'good life' is, naturally, changing over time and depending on its cultural context. This perception precedes the assessment of what is to be considered a virtue.

When talking about professions, the idea of 'good life' might appear out of line. Alasdair MacIntyre, a virtue ethicist on whom Chesterman builds his argument, relates *virtues* to human *practices,* which he defines as any coherent and complex forms of socially determined cooperative human activities. Such activities yield inherent goods, whose realization is of benefit for all participants. Only participants with expertise in that practice can fully appreciate the quality of these goods. Inherent goods are realized by striving for *excellence* in that very practice (cf. MacIntyre 1987, p. 255). Thus, this striving for excellence would be the most important virtue in professional practice. Besides this top virtue Chesterman (2001) identifies five other virtues, which distinguish the actions of a 'good translator': *fairness, truthfulness, trustworthiness, empathy, courage,* and *determination. Fairness* will prevent the actor from making choices that are intentionally biased towards one or the other option. *Truthfulness* shall provide a decision that is as honest as possible. 'Empathy' is commonly understood as the ability to understand and share the feelings of our communication partners. Empathy enables us to put ourselves into somebody else's shoes. As a virtue, *empathy* can be essential for successful communication and helps to realize the value of *understanding*. *Courage* as a virtue will empower the actor to place his or her own interests at risk when performing the practice (one does not need to think as far as settings of conflict or crisis, where 'risk' may include death, striving for excellence in one's own practice may collide with others' strive for efficiency and may endanger future engagements). *Determination* contributes to achieving excellence, not to give up until a good solution is found. Of course, virtues are not all one needs to excel in any practice. Skills and competences are essential: in the case of interpreting, among others, linguistic and cultural knowledge, transfer competence, research skills, technical skills. However, they fall out of the realm of ethics.

Recalling Prunč's list of principles, i.e. of virtues necessary to build a democratic translation/interpreting culture – *cooperativeness, loyalty, transparency*, and *ecologicality* – we see a picture similar to the one we obtained from the comparison of the values above. Again, the concepts Chesterman presents are of an elementary nature, whereas Prunč's concepts appear as much more complex. On the one side, we find terminology leaning on traditions of ethics; on the other, terminology leaning on modern discourse in politics, economics, and ecology. In the case of Chesterman, the relations between virtues and values are also clear, even though these relations are more complex than the preceding paragraph might suggest: there is no one-to-one relation between virtues and values. It might take a combination of virtues to realize a certain value, and a given virtue can be necessary for the realization of several values (see samples in Hebenstreit 2017). In the case of Prunč it is not so easy to relate virtues to individual values. It seems that *cooperativeness, loyalty, transparency*, and *ecologicality* must interact at all times.

Based on the available texts, it is not possible to perform a more comprehensive conceptual analysis of the two authors' conceptual systems that might clarify boundaries, areas of overlap or blank spaces in both models. However, the main problem for such an analysis would be that Chesterman and Prunč pursue different goals when writing about translation and interpreting ethics. The main difference I see in that sense is that Chesterman focuses on translation/interpreting ethics as professional ethics. Thus, he focuses on the moral values that professional translators and interpreters comply with (or should comply with) when they are hired for translation or interpreting assignments. Prunč's agenda goes far beyond that. A translation/interpreting culture is not limited to professional translation and interpreting. Professional translation/interpreting will most likely occupy most of the space in a translation/interpreting culture, it will be the central subsystem (and have its own subsystems), and this is the subsystem that Prunč most often refers to. However, it is not the only one. When Prunč talks about constructing a translation/interpreting culture, about negotiating consensus about conventions and norms, he talks about an endeavor that entails activities that lie outside the boundaries set by individual translation/interpreting assignments.

While Chesterman has tried to formulate a professional oath for translators, Prunč proposes a maxim for professional translators/interpreters that is based on *cooperativeness, loyalty, transparency,* and *ecologicality.* Chesterman's proposal reads as follows (Chesterman 2001, p. 153):

1. I swear to keep this Oath to the best of my ability and judgement. [Commitment]
2. I swear to be a loyal member of the translators' profession, respecting its history. I am willing to share my expertise with colleagues and to pass it on to trainee translators. I will not work for unreasonable fees. I will always translate to the best of my ability. [Loyalty to the profession]
3. I will use my expertise to maximize communication and minimize misunderstanding across language barriers. [Understanding]
4. I swear that my translations will not represent their source texts in unfair ways. [Truth]
5. I will respect my readers by trying to make my translations as accessible as possible, according to the conditions of each translation task. [Clarity]
6. I undertake to respect the professional secrets of my clients and not to exploit clients' information for personal gain. I promise to respect deadlines and to follow clients' instructions. [Trustworthiness]
7. I will be honest about my own qualifications and limitations; I will not accept work that is outside my competence. [Truthfulness]
8. I will inform clients of unresolved problems, and agree to arbitration in cases of dispute. [Justice]
9. I will do all I can to maintain and improve my competence, including all relevant linguistic, technical and other knowledge and skills. [Striving for excellence]

Prunč's proposal, on the other hand:

> "Act loyally to your action partners, but also have the self-confidence to demand their loyalty, use both your own and your partners' resources economically and consider the sustainability of your actions, act professionally and protect the reputation of your profession, act in compliance with the norms of your translation/interpreting culture, but have the courage, to act against these norms on your own responsibility and to lay open the reasons for your decision."[7] (Prunč 2012, p. 357-358) [My translation.]

Chesterman's Hieronymic oath is explicitly drafted before the background of various codes of ethics. Therefore it shares the bullet-point character of a number of such codes (for a critical assessment of such codes of ethics see Mulayim and Lai 2017, p. 54-58). One of the problems is that such rules do not provide any way out in cases of conflicting rules creating moral dilemmas. Prunč's maxim does provide such an option. It does not replace the contents of professional codes of practice or of a professional oath, which are assumed to exist in any given translation/interpreting culture. While Chesterman's proposal aims at a universally applicable professional oath (Chesterman 2001, p. 152), which has garnered quite some criticism, Prunč restricts his proposal to European translation/interpreting cultures, and is very skeptical about the possibility of a global translation/interpreting culture (2012, p. 358-359).

Conclusion

Prunč's conceptualization of *translation/interpreting culture* can serve as a very flexible framework for the study of translation and interpreting. It allows for an incredibly wide range of aspects to be integrated as elements of a specific translation/interpreting culture. Its nature is systemic and dynamic. As long as one accepts the idea of 'norm' in its various forms, approaches can be normative, descriptive, critical, or even activist. Professional ethics certainly constitute important elements of translation/interpreting cultures. However, although Prunč speaks of *translation/interpreting culture* as a

---

[7] "Handle loyal zu deinen Handlungspartnern, habe jedoch auch das Selbstbewusstsein, deren Loyalität einzufordern, gehe sparsam mit deinen und den Ressourcen deiner Partner um und bedenke die Nachhaltigkeit deiner Handlungen, handle professionell und wahre das Ansehen deines Berufsstandes, handle im Einklang mit den Normen deiner Translationskultur, habe jedoch den Mut, dich selbstverantwortlich dagegen zu entscheiden und die Gründe dafür offen zu legen."

'deontic' system and places it at the center of his reflections on translation ethics, I would not call *translation/interpreting culture* a proper system of morals, because it contains various kinds of norms that are not moral in nature. Thus, translation/interpreting ethics as sets of moral norms related to translation/interpreting act as constituents of translation/interpreting cultures. The conception of *translation/interpreting culture* as a subsystem of culture that can form further subsystems fits well with the general ethical conception of morals as group morals. Today's professional world is characterized by constant diversification and hybridization of professional profiles, giving birth to new translation/interpreting subcultures with potentially differing moral systems, not to mention non-professional subcultures.

Prunč's concept *translation/interpreting culture* is in itself not a conceptual tool for the analysis of translation/interpreting ethics. Its strength as a conceptual framework lies in its possibility to relate various elements to each other. Interrelatedness and multidirectionality (e.g. in the shape of 'reciprocity') appear to be the major characteristics from a methodological point of view. This strength, however, bears in itself a certain weakness. The four central principles *cooperativeness*, *loyalty*, *transparency*, and *ecologicality* may be used as conceptual tools, but appear so strongly interrelated that it might be difficult to operationalize these concepts for empirical purposes when analyzing moral issues in translation/interpreting. Prunč's emphasis on multidirectionality prepares the ground for multilateral loyalty and makes the translator/interpreter not only subject to moral obligations, but also subject to moral rights. This is, all in all, an important contribution towards empowering translators/ interpreters on the ethical frontier.

References

Chesterman, Andrew, 1997. Ethics of Translation. *In:* Mary Snell-Hornby, Zuzana Jettmarová & Klaus Kaindl, eds. *Translation as Intercultural Communication*. Amsterdam, Philadelphia: John Benjamins, 147-157.

———, 2001. Proposal for a Hieronymic Oath. *The Translator*, 7(2), 139-154.

———, 2004. Translation as an Object of Research. *In:* Harald Kittel, Armin Paul Frank, Norbert Greiner, Theo Hermans, Werner Koller, José Lambert & Fritz Paul, eds. *Übersetzung. Translation. Traduction. Ein internationales Handbuch zur Übersetzungsforschung. An International Encyclopedia of Translation Studies. Encyclopédie internationale de la recerche sur la traduction*. Berlin, New Yok: Walter der Gruyter, 93-100.

Cronin, Michael, 1998. The Cracked Looking Glass of Servants. *The Translator*, 4(2), 145-162.

Hebenstreit, Gernot, 2010. Berufskodizes als Konstituenten einer Translationsethik? Versuch einer Modellierung. *In:* Nadja Grbić, Gernot

Hebenstreit, Gisella Vorderobermeier & Michaela Wolf, eds. *Translationskultur Revisited.* Graz: Stauffenburg, 281-295.

———, 2017. Justice as a Guiding Principle? Considering ethical values underlying working principles for interpreters in asylum hearings. *In:* Esther Monzó & Juan Jiménez Salcedo, eds. *Les llengües minoritzades en l'ordre postmonolingüe.* Castelló de la Plana: Universitat Jaume I, 5-14.

Holz-Mänttäri, Justa, 1984. Translatorisches Handeln. Theorie und Methode.

MacIntyre, Alasdair, 1987. *Der Verlust der Tugend. Zur moralischen Krise der Gegenwart* translated by Wolfgang Riehl. Frankfurt am Main: Campus.

Mulayim, Sedat & Miranda Lai, 2017. *Ethics for Police Translators and Interpreters.* Boca Raton: CRC Press.

Nida-Rümelin, Julian, 2005. Theoretische und angewandte Ethik: Paradigmen, Begründungen, Bereiche Alfred Kröner. *In:* Julian Nida-Rümelin, ed. *Angewandte Ethik.* Stuttgart: Alfred Kröner, 2-87.

Pieper, Annemarie, 2007. *Einführung in die Ethik.* Tübingen, Basel: A. Francke.

Prunč, Erich, 1997. Translationskultur (Versuch einer konstruktiven Kritik des translatorischen Handelns) ['Translation and Interpreting Culture (attempting a constructive critique of translational action)']. *TEXTconTEXT*, 11(2), 99-127.

———, 2000a. Translation in die Nicht-Muttersprache und Translationskultur. *In:* Meta Grosman, Mira Kadrić, Irena Kovačič & Mary Snell-Hornby, eds. *Translation into non-mother tongues.* Tübingen: Stauffenburg, 5-20.

———, 2000b. Vom Translationsbiedermeier zur Cyber-translation. *TEXTconTEXT*, 14(1), 3-74.

———, 2001. Quod licet Iovi ... *TEXTconTEXT*, 15(2), 165-179.

———, 2002. Translation zwischen Absolutheitsansprüchen und Konventionen. *In:* Lew Zybatow, ed. *Translation zwischen Theorie und Praxis.* Frankfurt am Main: Lang, 139-166.

———, 2005a. Hypothesen zum Gattungsprofil deutsch-slowenischer Übersetzungen im Zeitraum 1848-1918. *In:* Nike Kocijančič Pokorn, ed. *Beyond equivalence.* Graz: Karl-Franzens-Univ. Graz, 19-37.

———, 2005b. Translationsethik. *In:* Peter Sandrini, ed. *Fluctuat nec mergitur.* Frankfurt am Main: Lang, 165-194.

———, 2005c. Translationsethik. Translation ethics. *Informatologia*, 38(1-2), 9-21.

———, 2005d. Zwischen Welten und Werten. Identitätskonstruktionen in Ward Justs *The Translator.* *In:* Ingrid Kurz & Klaus Kaindl, eds. *Wortklauber, Sinnverdreher, Brückenbauer?* Wien: Lit, 153-163.

———, 2008. Zur Konstruktion von Translationskulturen. *In:* Larisa Schippel, ed. *Translationskultur – ein innovatives und produktives Konzept.* Berlin: Frank & Timme, 19-41.

———, 2012. *Entwicklungslinien der Translationswissenschaft. Von den Asymmetrien der Sprachen zu den Asymmetrien der Macht.* 3 ed. Berlin: Frank & Timme.

Reiß, Katharina & Hans Josef Vermeer, 1984. *Grundlegung einer allgemeinen Translationstheorie.* 2 ed. Tübingen: Niemeyer.

Schippel, Larisa, ed. 2008. *Translationskultur: ein innovatives und produktives Konzept,* Berlin: Frank & Timme.

Schreiber, Michael, 2011. Erich Prunč. Entwicklungslinien der Translationswissenschaft. Von den Asymmetrien der Sprachen zu den Asymmetrien der Macht. *Target,* 22(2), 391-396.

Schweppenhäuser, Gerhard, 2003. *Grundbegriffe der Ethik zur Einführung.* Hamburg: Junius.

Syrjänen, Niina, 2014. Translation Culture in the Military: Russian-speakers in the Finnish land forces during the Second World War. *In:* Tamara Mikolič, Kaisa Koskinen & Nike Kocijančič-Pokorn, eds. *New horizons in translation research and education 2.* Joensuu: University of Eastern Finland, 90-108.

Venuti, Lawrence, 1998. *The Scandals of Translation. Towards an ethics of difference.* London: Routledge.

Wolf, Michaela, 2010. Translationskultur versus Translationsfeld? Zu den 'Spielregeln' translatorischer Funktionsweisen. *In:* Nadja Grbić, Gernot Hebenstreit, Gisella Vorderobermeier & Michaela Wolf, eds. *Translationskultur revisited. Festschrift für Erich Prunč.* Tübingen: Stauffenberg, 21-32.

Chapter 5

Translation and climate justice: Minority perspectives

Michael Cronin

This chapter explores the relationships between climate justice and translation reviewing conventional ideas on translation and the environment. By exposing the effects of implementing seemingly harmless choices, it stresses how non-human beings and human minorities have been marginalized and their interests silenced in order to privilege the gains of the powerful. The chapter presents how political decisions (generally and in specific cases) have resulted in communicative and environmental losses affecting both dominant and dominated communities. It further stresses the need for an ethics of translation that goes beyond major human languages and focuses on understanding minoritized human and non-human communities.

It is an old story but, in our context, one worth repeating. In the months leading up to the lunar landing, the *Apollo 11* astronauts trained in a remote, moon-like desert in the western United States. The area is home to a number of Native American communities and, one day, the astronauts came across an elderly Native American. When they explained what they were doing, the old man asked them if they could do him a favor. They said they would if they could. The elder explained that his people believed that holy spirits lived on the moon and he wanted to pass on a message from his people. He gave the astronauts the message in his tribal language and asked them to memorize it by heart:

"What does it mean?", asked the astronauts.

"Oh, I cannot tell you. It's a secret that only our tribe and the moon spirits are allowed to know."

When they got back from the moon, the astronauts searched the base until they could find someone who could translate the secret message. When they repeated what they had memorized, the translator started laughing and could not stop. When eventually he did, he explained that the sentence they had so carefully committed to memory could be translated as, "Don't believe a single word these people are telling you. They have come to steal your lands."

This story is less important for its truth value than for the well-known anxieties around colonization and dispossession. The colonizer speaks with a forked tongue and what he says is rarely what he means. There is, of course, another dimension to this story bound up with translation and minority languages. The language of the astronauts and the language of the Native American are radically asymmetrical in terms of access to status and resources. Only non-translation can allow for a temporary displacement of power to the Native American language but is only translation which allows for the uncomfortable truths of colonial encounters to be communicated to wider audiences. It is translation which, in effect, translates the tendentiousness of the colonizers' words of greeting.

Arran Stibbe, towards the end of his work on the emerging discipline of ecolinguistics, makes the following observation:

> There is, however, a shortage of voices, in this book and in ecolinguistics in general, from traditional and indigenous cultures around the world. Within these cultures are a great multitude of stories, some of which may be invaluable in the reinvention of self and society in the transition to new ways of living and being. (Stibbe 2015, p. 193)

The importance of "traditional and indigenous cultures" is not simply to do with past stories as a source of future change but with present stories as a pointer to imminent survival. Naomi Klein notes that running economies on energy sources that release poisons into the atmosphere as an inescapable part of their extraction and refining has always necessitated the existence of "sacrifice zones." These zones have a number of features in common:

> They were poor places. Out-of-the-way places. Places where residents lacked political power, usually having to do with some combination of race, language, and class. And the people who lived in these condemned places knew they had been written off. (Klein 2014, p. 310)

It is often the poorest people on the planet speaking lesser-used languages in more remote parts of the world that find themselves at the frontline of the race to extract as much fossil fuel resources as possible from the earth. Describing how the Beaver Lake Cree Nation took on oil and gas companies over tar sands oil extraction, Klein claims that "some of the most marginalized people in my country are [...] taking on some of the most wealthiest and most powerful people on the planet" (Klein 2014, p. 379). The move to a carbon credits system, a market solution that allows wealthier countries and corporations to offset carbon emissions by buying carbon *credits* from countries with low emissions, has made the situation of indigenous peoples even more precarious. Bram Brüscher, a geographer, has coined the term "liquid nature" to describe the way in which fields, forests and mountains lose their intrinsic, place-based meaning and become deracinated, abstract commodities in a global trading system (Büscher 2013, p. 20-36). In the Bajo Aguán region of Honduras, owners of palm oil plantations have been able to register a carbon offset project that they claim captures methane. Encouraged by the promise of financial gain from captured gas, huge tree farms have disrupted and displaced local agriculture. A resulting violent cycle of evictions and land occupations had by 2013 led to the deaths of up to a hundred local farmers and their advocates (Wong 2013). As Klein remarks, "it's easier to cordon off a forest inhabited by politically weak people in a poor country than to stop politically powerful corporate emitters in rich countries" (Klein 2014, p. 223). An additional irony is that it is indigenous peoples practicing some of the most sustainable, low-carbon lifestyles on the planet who are being sacrificed for the carbon market.

One way of articulating the connection between climate change and the challenge of extractives is through the notion of climate justice. This is defined by the Mary Robinson Foundation - Climate Justice as follows:

> Climate Justice links human rights and development to achieve a human-centred approach, safeguarding the rights of the most vulnerable and sharing the burdens and benefits of climate change and its resolution equitably and fairly. Climate justice is informed by science, responds to science and acknowledges the need for equitable stewardship of the world's resources. (Mary Robinson Foundation 2017)

The Global Justice Ecology Project argues in starker terms:

> Climate change may well be humanity's greatest challenge. It is a crisis that must be rapidly addressed if catastrophe is to be averted. Already the impacts are being felt by millions in the world's most vulnerable and marginalised communities. Climate Change is at once a social and environmental justice issue, an ecological issue, and an issue of economic and political domination. (Global Justice Ecology Project 2017)

Clearly, a core connection is between social and economic marginalization and environmental impacts. The question is how are we to know or understand what these impacts are and what is the extent of the cultural, social and economic disruption as a result of climate change? The Global Justice Ecology Project tells us that, "Indigenous Peoples, peasant communities, fisherfolk, and especially women in these communities, have been able to live harmoniously and sustainably with the Earth for millennia," but how do we know this? In the Principles of Climate Justice as enunciated by the Mary Robinson Foundation we are told that "the opportunity to participate in decision-making processes which are fair, accountable, open and corruption-free is essential to the growth of a culture of climate justice. The voices of the most vulnerable to climate change must be heard and acted upon", but again the question that might be asked is, how are we to hear these voices and how are we to act upon them? As is obvious from the leading questions, the answers lie in the dispiritingly obvious, language and translation. If Translation Studies has ignored climate justice as a core concern of its fields of enquiry, the literature around climate justice equally pays scant attention to the question of minority or minoritized languages and translation.

In the case of the literature on climate justice, it is worth reflecting for a moment on the reason for this indifference. The indifference is ironically bound up with the extractives logic that the pioneers of climate justice would so vocally decry. Pascal Chabot, in his *L'âge des transitions* (2015), has argued for the development of the new discipline or interdiscipline of 'transitology', the science and art of moving to more sustainable, resilient and viable economies and societies in order to avoid the irrevocable destruction of the ecosystem. The Belgian philosopher argues that there is a persistent taboo around the making explicit of energy sources in our society, from the silence of Greek philosophy on the subject of slave labor to the marginal presence of fossil fuels in the modern novel. This is part of what Chabot calls the *boîte noire*, the Black Box of concealment where the activities of the extractive industries are hidden from public view and critique. This leads in turn to what Chabot, however, calls the elitism of means over ends. As the Indian leader, Mahatma Gandhi, once remarked, there is no road to peace, peace is the road. In other words, Chabot is skeptical about forms of political debates that are excessively focused on *values* in the form of societal ends. It would generally be hard to find a party anywhere in the world that did not profess a belief at some level in democracy, equality, and justice. Consensus about ends is widespread. And for that reason, increasingly meaningless. The real differences emerge in the means used to realize those ends. Political struggle shifts from a conflict around the preeminence of ends to a rivalry around the appropriateness of means. A society can agree that it is a good idea for its citizens to move about freely, so free movement is an end, but how? Petrol-driven private cars? Airplanes? Helicopters? Public transport? Trams? Cars? Bicycles? Depending on the choices made, roads are built or abandoned, railway lines are laid down or pulled up, cyclists live or die, pedestrians get to work or lie in intensive care, health expenditure rises or falls. If means, such as fossil fuels, have changed the world, the logic is that changing the world involves changing the means. It is in this context that translation takes on a particular importance as translation is preeminently the *means* used to bring a work of literature into another culture, to sell a product to speakers of a different language or to convey a body of thought or set of beliefs into a foreign setting. The ontological fixation and the privileging of ends over means must explain, in part, the long recorded marginalization of translation practice in the West (Venuti 2008). Thus, there is little point in professing an interest in dialogue or issuing an invitation to participate in decision-making processes if there is a revealing silence on the means that will allow this to happen, namely, through translation and a meaningful engagement with minoritized languages. If justice is also a means to arrive at commonly agreed ends (equity, security, physical integrity) any discussion of justice in a plurilingual world must engage with the linguistic means that facilitate or complicate the juridical means. In what follows, we will consider three different scenarios that point up a connection between climate justice, translation and minority languages.

Scenario one

The first scenario comes from the Kimberley region in Western Australia. This is the region that enjoys the greatest linguistic diversity in all of Australia. Of the thirty languages in the region, only three are spoken by children. Hall Creek shire is a part of Kimberley that has become a meeting point for most of the languages in the region. The reason for this was twofold. Firstly, black children from all over Kimberley were deported to a cattle station and "Native Welfare Station" called Moola Bulla. Secondly, the arrival of mining to the area meant the establishment of a town straddling the border between unrelated tongues, Kija and Jaru. As Mark Abley points out, "now young speakers of other languages found themselves in the same area. The inevitable happened: a creole emerged. Today Kriol is the daily medium for the vast majority of Aboriginal people around Halls Creek" (Abley 2003, p. 35). In other words, what emerged in the translation zone of Halls Creek was a spontaneously generated language that attempted to deal with the translation aporias of language contact. The Kriol is as much an artifact of translation as it is an admission of the impossibility of translation in such a linguistically charged setting.

Anna Tsing in an essay entitled "Blasted Landscapes (and the Gentle art of Mushroom Picking)" looks at the various histories of environmental destruction and disturbance that have led to the growth of a variety of wild mushroom known as *matsutake*, which is much prized in Japan and elsewhere. She argues that "sites in which human and nonhuman histories of disturbance come together are particularly good to think with because such sites allow us to track humans as both vectors and victims of disturbance. This is a territory of unintended consequences for both humans and nonhumans" (Tsing 2014, p. 92). Halls Creek is a site of human and nonhuman disturbance. The human disturbance of the forcible deportation of Aboriginal children and the nonhuman disturbance of the local which takes the form of mining and the extractives industry. The emergence of Kriol is one of the unintended consequences of this disturbance regime, but another is the pressure that Kriol is exercising on the already weakened and endangered languages of the region which are increasingly only spoken and understood by the elders. Given the paucity of translation supports and language teaching resources for the indigenous languages of Kimberley and the dominance of English as the language of extractivism, the disturbance history of Halls Creek points to a bleak future for the linguistic diversity of the region. In 2016 the company Northern Minerals began mining in the area for heavy rare earth metals and other mining companies are actively prospecting for iron ore. The current Wikipedia entry for Halls Creek notes that "The commercial industry in the small town is expected to grow massively, with McDonalds, Woolworths, Coles, Kmart and many other stores planning to develop if the mining companies choose to mine in the surrounding area" (Wikipedia 2017). The absence of a concerted policy around translation and the preservation of bicultural diversity means that, in terms of climate justice, Halls Creek becomes in Naomi Klein's words, one of the planet's "sacrifice zones."

Scenario two

The second scenario is bound up with the minoritization of major languages through translation as a way of alerting speakers to justice issues around environmental degradation. The botanist Oliver Rackham in *The History of the Countryside* (2000) outlines four ways in which, in his words, the "landscape is lost" (2000, p. 14), through the loss of beauty, the loss of wildlife and vegetation, and the loss of meaning. For the travel and nature writer Robert Macfarlane, it is the loss of meaning that is particularly troubling. He claims that *Landmarks* is fundamentally, "a book about the power of language – strong style, single words – to shape our sense of place" (Macfarlane 2015,

p. 1). As words to describe specific aspects of landscape – land, sea, weather, atmosphere – begin to ebb from a major language like English, then the ability of English speakers to be able to see the world around them becomes fatally compromised. As Macfarlane puts it, "Language deficit leads to attention deficit" (2015, p. 24). Increasingly, he argues, "The nuances observed by specialized vocabularies are evaporating from common usage, burnt off by capital, apathy and urbanization. The terrain beyond the city fringe has become progressively more understood in terms of large generic units ('field,' 'hill,' 'valley,' 'wood'). It has become blandscape" (2015, p. 23). Macfarlane sets about compiling a "Counter-Desecration Phrasebook" with glossaries grouped under the headings of "Flatlands", "Uplands", "Waterlands", "Coastlands", "Underlands", "Northlands", "Edgelands", "Earthlands", "Woodlands" and one glossary left blank for the reader's own use. These glossaries in their coverage of the British landscape draw on "Norn and Old English, Anglo-Romani, Cornish, Welsh, Irish, Gaelic, the Orcadian, Shetlandic and Doric dialects of Scots, and numerous regional versions of English, through to the last vestiges of living Norman still spoken on the Channel Islands" (2015, p. 1). What is striking about the glossaries is the extent to which the minority languages of Britain and minoritized varieties of English (regional versions of English) itself become central to this process of the recovery of landscape from lexical abandonment. In other words, the loss of meaning Rackham describes and which is repeatedly emphasized by Macfarlane in his own travels in the book and through the travelling of others show how a major language can become in a sense *minoritized* through the shrinkage of its lexical range and semantic reach. In the edition of the *Oxford Junior Dictionary* that came out in 2007, Macfarlane notes words that were deleted included, "acorn, adder, ash, beech, bluebell, buttercup, catkin, conker, cowslip, cygnet, dandelion, fern, hazel, heather, heron, ivy, kingfisher, lark, mistletoe, nectar, newt, otter, pasture and willow" (2015, p. 3). Reversing this loss of description and reference involves admitting two forms of minority to the major language, the word-hoard of Britain's different minority languages, and the multiple dialect forms of English throughout the island. The major language as it excludes language minority becomes increasingly unable to describe the natural and physical world in which its speakers dwell. The opacity of the world reveals the impoverished descriptive hubris of a language that loses more insights as it gains more speakers.

Ignoring the minority reports of English and other languages has implications beyond a poverty of description. A failure to see means a failure to see a great many things and not just the landscape before you. McFarlane in describing his reactions to Barry Lopez's travel writings, *Arctic Dreams*, claims that one of the lessons the book taught him was that, "while writing about landscape often begins in the aesthetic it ends in the ethical." Lopez's intense attentiveness was "a form of moral gaze born of his belief that if we attend more closely to something then we are less likely to act more selfishly towards it" (2015, p. 211). In other words, attending to lexis is a matter not of nostalgia but of urgency. The American poet and farmer Wendell Berry sees language as a way forward, not a step backwards:

> People *exploit* what they have merely concluded to be of value, but they *defend* what they love and to defend what we love we need a particularizing language, for we love what we particularly know. (Berry 2000, p. 41)

What this might mean politically is illustrated by the responses to a proposal submitted by an engineering company AMEC supported by British Energy for the development of a wind farm on Brindled Moor on the Isle of Lewis in the Outer Hebrides. The proposal consisted of a wind "power station" of 234 turbines each 140 meters high with a blade span of 80 meters (the terminology of "farm" tries to mask the reality: these installations are dispersed power stations). Each turbine required a foundation of 700 cubic meters of concrete and "5 million cubic metres of rock and 2.5 million cubic metres of peat would be excavated and displaced" (Macfarlane 2015, p. 28). One response was the publication of a booklet *A-mach an Gleann/A Known Wilderness* where the co-authors, Anne Campbell and Jon McLeod mapped their moor-walks, describing in great detail features of landscape, wildlife, folk memory that they observed or remembered on the way. The second was the compilation by Anne Campbell and Finlay McLeod of *Some Lewis Moorland Terms: A Peat Glossary*, glossary of 126 Gaelic terms to describe features of the moorland such as *teine biorach*, "the flame or the will-o'-the-wisp that runs on the top of heather when the moor is burnt during the summer" or a *rùdhan*, "set of four peat blocks leaned up against one another such that the wind helps their drying" (Macfarlane 2015, p. 18). The terms here are in Scots Gaelic, but in the glossary at the end of the second chapter discussing the moorland controversy, there are English dialect words from Sussex, Yorkshire, Essex, Exmoor, Northamptonshire, Somerset, Suffolk, Cumbria, East Anglia and the West Country. What the *Peat Glossary* and *A Known Wilderness* are contesting is the notion of the moorland as a *terra nullius*, ripe for development and extraction. When James Carnegy-Arbuthnot, an estate owner in Angus argued in 2013 that it was right that so few people own most of the land in Scotland because most of it was "unproductive wilderness," he was readily equating emptiness of landscape and plenitude of possession. What the excluded languages – minority languages outside and within English – do is to restore a sense of history, particularity, complexity and (common) ownership to place. Noteworthy in the responses to the AMEC development is that travel and language – the moor-walks and the glossary – are both intertwined in opposition to the proposed project and detailed and loving description of place becomes inescapably ethical. In a broader sense, what the strategic minoritization of the major languages of industrial development through involves is an overall shift from what Naomi Klein calls an ideology of extractivism to an ideology of regeneration. A regenerative move that challenges through the energies of minority and minoritized major languages the neo-colonial and predatory emptying out of landscape and language.

Scenario three

The third scenario is the least expected in terms of the conventional assumptions we make around translation and minority issues. In an interview prior to the COP21 conference in Paris, Mary Robinson, articulated what she saw as a key focus of climate justice, "Climate change can be difficult to communicate. It is often seen as distant and highly technical, Climate justice focuses our attention on people, rather than ice-caps and greenhouse gases. I think this makes the threat of climate change more tangible" (Canzi 2016). What appears like a good communications strategy is, however, deeply flawed as a form of interpretation and indeed may become complicit in exacerbating the very problem it wants to address. From Dipesh Chakrabarty's notion of deep history to Michel Serre's idea of the *grand récit*, a common thread in thinking in the age of the Anthropocene is the notion that the fates of the human and the non-human worlds are inextricably bound up with each other (Serres 2003; Chakrabarty 2009). It is no longer possible to postulate an anthropocentric, hierarchical order where the non-human world is passively subject to the interventions and manipulations of the human subject. The non-human is striking back. The Annual Statement of the World Meteorological Organization on the State of the Global Climate issued on 21 March 2017 confirmed that 2016 was the warmest year on record, $1.1°C$ above the pre-industrial period and $0.06°$ C above the previous record for 2016. Globally averaged sea surface temperatures were the warmest on record. Global sea levels continued to rise, reaching record highs. In November 2016 alone, global sea-ice extent dropped more than four million square kilometers below average. In 2015 carbon dioxide levels in the atmosphere breached the symbolic landmark of 400 parts per million (World Meteorological Organization 2017). Geological and human history converge. The Great Story that stretches from the Big Bang to the emergence of Homo Sapiens is not one that has the teleological purpose of human survival. The more humans ignore the non-human world, the less likely it is to ignore them. The result is that the

Earth will endure but that there is no necessary reason why earthlings – agents and victims of increasingly destructive environmental behavior – will. In other words, the difficulty with the anthropocentric focus of climate justice is that it replicates the ideology of human exceptionalism which is at the origin of the current ecological crisis. When the only things that matter or are valued are those things that matter to humans then the structures humans elaborate will routinely ignore the non-human. Thomas Berry, the cultural historian notes that, "our legal system fosters a sense of human rights, with other-than-human beings having no inherent rights" (1999, p. 102). Since Berry wrote those words, scholars have begun to consider the question of environmental justice particularly in the area of political theory and philosophy (Schlosberg 2009; Walker 2011; Sikor 2013; Martin 2017). Notwithstanding this interest we still have Human Rights Watch but no organization called Non-Human Rights Watch. If the American constitution, for example, guarantees humans participatory government, individual freedoms and the right to own and dispose of property, there is no protection for the natural world. As Berry has argued, "Only a jurisprudence based on a concern for an integral Earth community is capable of sustaining a viable planet" (1999, p. 74). Thinking of mountains, rivers or forests as independent legal entities possessing inalienable rights poses considerable challenges for routine ways of conceiving of law and justice. In May 2015, at the initiative of Bruno Latour and Laurence Tubiana, a simulation was enacted in the *Théâtre des Amandiers* in Paris. Anticipating the discussions at in Paris in December a group of students from around thirty different countries acted out roles as part of different delegations. They were, however, delegations with a difference. There were, of course, delegations from 'France' and 'India' and 'Australia' but there were also delegations from 'Forests' and 'Oceans' and 'Atmosphere.' Bruno Latour is alive to the difficulties implicit in these experimental forms of jurisprudence but claims:

> Si vous étonnez qu'on fasse parler « forêt », alors il faut vous étonner aussi qu'un président parle comme représentant de « France ». Personne morale pour personne morale chacune a beaucoup à dire et ne s'exprime que par une vertigineuse série d'indispensables truchements.[1] (Latour 2015, p. 339)

---

[1] "If you are surprised to see 'Forest' given a voice, then you have to be just as surprised that a president speaks as the representative of 'France.' Each corporate body has a good deal to say, and each can express itself only through a dizzying series of indispensable mediations/translations" (Latour 2017)

The good governance of water, soil and air demands at the very least representative government and that representation implies a "dizzying series of indispensable mediations/translations." Put simply, there is no representation without translation. If a transversal form of post-anthropocentric subjectivity is to emerge, it demands that we think about the languages, the forms of communication, the signifying systems of the non-human and how we are to translate forms of intelligibility that allowed for the shared sovereignty of the planet. If non-human presence has been spectacularly minoritized by Cartesian dualism and the Christian doctrine of the soul, notions of climate justice and translation need to move beyond the strict purview of the human if they are not to be complicit in ecologically damaging forms of subjection.

A further dimension to this question is the plight of living organisms with whom we share the planet. The relationship between humans and other species has featured prominently in debates in both the Anglophone and the Francophone worlds. It is the question of *animalité* that has exercised the minds of French thinkers such as Vinciane Despret, Élisabeth de Fontenay, Dominique Lestel and Aymeric Caron in the last number of decades (Lestel 1996; de Fontenay 1997; Despret 2007; Caron 2017). Their concerns have been as much with the question of animal rights that have been to the fore in the Anglophone world as with the notion of human as animal and our relationship as organisms with other members of the animal kingdom. Jean-Marie Schaeffer, for example, in his *La Fin de l'exception humaine* (2007) argues for the need to end human exceptionalism and recognize the embeddedness of humans in the physical world. Schaeffer draws on work in cognitive psychology and neurosciences to develop a non-reductionist continuism. He argues that literary studies, for example, need to work from a more 'integrationist' notion of human that includes a concept of human as developed in ethology, anthropology, evolutionary psychology and cognitive science.

De-centering human perspectives, deconstructing the animal/human binary that is part of the legacy of Cartesian dualism does not mean denying difference or arguing for some form of biological reductionism (humans can be reduced to their biological, animal self) but it is a refusal to fetishize difference. The insistence on what we do not have in common with animals systematically overlooks what we do have in common. It precisely this question of difference and similarity and what the implications might be for justice that has engaged thinkers in the English-speaking world even if they have, to date, evinced no interest in the question or necessity of translation (Corbey 2005; Donaldson and Kymlicka 2013; Suddendorf 2013). The predicament of the non-human is all the more dramatic in that we are living through what Elisabeth Kolbert has called the sixth extinction where animal species are being destroyed at an unprecedented rate (Kolbert 2014). The natural *background* rate of species extinction is about one to five species a year. However, species currently estimate we are losing species at 1,000 to 10,000 times the background rate. This means that between 30 and 50 percent of all species will be extinct by mid-century. The situation of domesticated animals is scarcely better. There are one billion domesticated pigs, 1.5 billion cows and 20 billion chickens on the planet and the vast majority are subject to the brutalizing regimes of industrialized farming (Harari 2011). As the historian Yuval Noah Harari has pointed out:

> This is why the fate of farm animals is not an ethical side issue. It concerns the majority of Earth's large creatures: tens of billions of sentient beings, each with a complex world of sensations and emotions, but which live and die on an industrial production line. (Harari 2015)

Again, what is implicit in Harari's comments is an ethics of translation. How are we to know that our fellow creatures have a "complex world of sensations and emotions" if we do not attempt to translate what they are experiencing into forms of meaning that are intelligible to humans? If the majority of sentient beings on this planet find themselves ruthlessly minoritized in industrialised routines of life and death, is it not time that we expand the remit of what is understood by intersemiotic translation to include various forms of animal communication, on which there is now an extensive body of research (see Slobodchikoff 2012)? If part of the struggle for justice in the colonial period was to give voice through translation to the oppression of the subaltern, to turn the colonised from positivistic objects of commercial exploitation and scientific enquiry to hermeneutic subjects of sentient experience and liberation (Cronin 2006), then Translation Studies might finally turn its attention to the minoritized languages of the majority of beings on the planet. We might not be comfortable with what they have to say, but we need to hear it before it is too late.

During the Versailles negotiations in April 1919, the American President Woodrow Wilson was keen to propose a special treaty that would link Poland's membership of the League of Nations to a commitment to bestow equal treatment on racial and national minorities. Philippe Sands, Professor of Law at University College London, described the aghast reaction of the British delegation who were fearful similar rights would be accorded to "American Negroes, Southern Irish, Flemings and Catalans" (Sands 2016, p. 72). Another official complained that the League of Nations should not be allowed to protest minorities or it would have "the right to protect the Chinese in

Liverpool, the Roman Catholics in France, the French in Canada, quite apart from more serious problems such as the Irish" (2016, p. 72). Francis argues that the debates around the treatment of minorities at the Versailles conference would eventually lead to the formulation of a number of basic principles of international humanitarian law. Significantly, the jurist who would eventually formulate the notion of *crimes against humanity*, Ralph Lauterpacht, worked at the conference not in his legal capacity (he was too young) but as an interpreter. If humanity is once again in trouble, the question of minority must once more be addressed. Climate justice is an attempt to do this, but arguably the attempt will fail if there is not a fuller engagement with the implications of language and translation for any sense of global ecological equity. To return to the tale of the Apollo 11 crew, we do not want to be in a situation where no one believes a word we say because we fail to understand what they are saying or where they do, but it is too late because the lands have already been stolen and the planet with it.

References

Abley, Mark, 2003. *Spoken Here: Travels Among Threatened Languages*. London: Heinemann.

Berry, Thomas M., 1999. *The Great Work*. New York: Bell Tower.

Berry, Wendell, 2000. *Life is a Miracle*. Berkeley: Counterpoint Press.

Büscher, Bram, 2013. Nature on the move: the value and circulation of liquid nature and the emergence of fictitious conservation. *New Proposals: Journal of Marxism and Interdisciplinary Enquiry*, 6(1-2), 20-36.

Canzi, Germana, 2016. Q&A with Mary Robinson: What is Climate Justice?'. *The Road to Paris*. Online: http://roadtoparis.info/2015/07/29/qa-with-mary-robinson-what-is-climate-justice/.

Caron, Aymeric, 2017. *Antispéciste*. Paris: Seuil.

Chabot, Patrick, 2015. *L'âge des transitions*. Paris: PUF.

Chakrabarty, Dipesh, 2009. The Climate of History: Four Theses. *Critical Inquiry*, 35(2), 197-222.

Corbey, Raymond, 2005. *The Metaphysics of Apes: negotiating the animal-human boundary*. Cambridge: Cambridge University Press.

Cronin, Michael, 2006. *Translation and Identity*. London: Routledge.

Despret, Vinciane, 2007. *Bêtes et hommes*. Paris: Gallimard.

Donaldson, Sue & Will Kymlicka, 2013. *Zoopolis: A Political Theory of Animal Rights*. Oxford: Oxford University Press.

de Fontenay, Élisabeth, 1997. *Le Silence des bêtes: la philosophie à l'épreuve de l'animalité*. Paris: Fayard.

Global Justice Ecology Project, 2017. *Climate Justice*. Online: https://globaljusticeecology.org/climate-justice/.

Harari, Yuval Noah, 2011. *Sapiens: A Brief History of Mankind*. London: Vintage Books.

———, 2015. Industrialised farming one of the worst crimes in history, *The Guardian*. Online: https://www.theguardian.com/books/2015/sep/25/industrial-farming-one-worst-crimes-history-ethical-question.

Klein, Naomi, 2014. *This Changes Everything: Capitalism vs. the Climate*. London: Allen Lane.

Kolbert, Elisabeth, 2014. *The Sixth Extinction: An Unnatural History*. London: Bloomsbury.

Latour, Bruno, 2015. *Face à Gaïa*. Paris: La Découverte.

———, 2017. *Facing Gaia. Eight Lectures on the New Climatic Regime*. translated by Catherine Porter. Cambridge: Polity.

Lestel, Domnique 1996. *L'Animalité, essai sur le statut de l'humain*. Paris: Hatier.

Macfarlane, Robert, 2015. *Landmarks*. London: Hamish Hamilton.

Martin, Adrian, 2017. *Just Conservation: Biodiversity, Wellbeing and Sustainability*. Abingdon: Routledge.

Mary Robinson Foundation, 2017. *Principles of Climate Justice*. Online: https://www.mrfcj.org/principles-of-climate-justice/.

Rackham, Oliver, 2000. *The History of the Countryside*. London: W&N.

Sands, Philippe, 2016. *East West Street*. London: W&N.

Schaeffer, Jean-Marie, 2007. *La fin de l'exception humaine*. Paris: Gallimard.

Schlosberg, David, 2009. *Defining Environmental Justice: theories, movements and nature*. Oxford: Oxford University Press.

Serres, Michel, 2003. *Hominescence*. Paris: Livre de Poche.

Sikor, Thomas, ed. 2013. *The Justices and Injustices of Ecosystem Services*, London: Routledge.

Slobodchikoff, Con, 2012. *Chasing Doctor Dolittle: Learning the Languages of Animals*. New York: St Martin's Press.

Stibbe, Arran, 2015. *Ecolinguistics: Language, Ecology and the Stories We Live By*. London: Routledge.

Suddendorf, Thomas, 2013. *The Gap: the science of what separates us from animals*. New York: Basic Books.

Tsing, Anna, 2014. Blasted Landscapes (and the Gentle Art of Mushroom Picking). Online: http://www.multispecies-salon.org/tsing/.

Venuti, Lawrence, 2008. *The Translator's Invisibility: a History of Translation*. London: Routledge.

Walker, Gordon, 2011. *Environmental Justice*. London: Routledge.

Wikipedia, 2017. *Halls Creek, Western Australia*. Online: https://en.wikipedia.org/wiki/Halls_Creek,_Western_Australia.

Wong, Rosi, 2013. The oxygen trade: leaving Hondurans gasping for air, *Foreign Policy in Focus*.

World Meterological Organization, 2017. *WMO Statement on the State of the Global Climate in 2017*. Online: https://public.wmo.int/en/wmo-statement-state-of-global-climate-2017.

Chapter 6

The role of indigenous interpreters in the Peruvian intercultural, bilingual justice system

Raquel de Pedro Ricoy,
Luis Andrade Ciudad & Rosaleen Howard

Since 2012, the Peruvian State, through its Ministry of Culture, has been training indigenous translators and interpreters. Their remit is to facilitate communication between the indigenous population of the country and its institutions, against a socio-political background of historical marginalization of, and discrimination against, indigenous peoples, their languages and cultures.

This paper is based on research and fieldwork conducted by the authors in Peru between October 2014 and June 2016.[1] It will focus specifically on the role that the indigenous interpreters play in guaranteeing access to justice for speakers of minoritized languages. Relevant contextual information about Peru will be provided, including the legal framework for the provision of interpreting services between Spanish and indigenous languages. The paper will further describe the training program put in place by the State, before critically addressing the challenges that practitioners and institutions face. We will also report on *ad hoc* interpreting initiatives that are beginning to emerge in the country, beyond the remit of the State training programs, and will conclude with some general observations derived from our research.

---

[1] The project, entitled "Translating Cultures: the legislated mediation of indigenous rights in Peru," was conducted between October 2014 and June 2016, in collaboration with the NGO Asociación Servicios Educativos Rurales as project partner, and was funded by the UK Arts and Humanities Research Council (AHRC, Award No. AH/M003566/1), for whose support we are grateful. We are also grateful to the Ministry of Culture of Peru for their valuable support in facilitating our access to interpreters, translators, State employees, and translator and interpreter trainers.

Introduction

Peru is a highly biodiverse, resource-rich country. In modern times, national and transnational companies are exploiting its reserves of minerals in the Andean region and oil and natural gas in the Amazon rainforest with ever increasing intensity. The country is home to a multi-ethnic population that comprises native peoples, as well as groups of European, African and Asian descent. According to *The Sociolinguistic Atlas of Indigenous Peoples in Latin America* (Sichra 2009), the native peoples make up 13.9% of the population and speak, as per government estimates, some 47 indigenous languages. According to the most recent legislation, to be discussed in what follows, the indigenous tongues have official status "in the areas where they predominate." (Indigenous Languages Act, 2011, Article 9, see Congress of the Republic of Peru 2011b). Spanish is the country's *lingua franca*. Yet, the Spanish spoken by indigenous bilinguals is highly stigmatized, both in Lima, the capital city and in the main localities of the Andes (Escobar 1978; De los Heros 1999; Cerrón-Palomino 2003; Zavala and Córdova 2010).

Against this complex and diverse ethnolinguistic landscape, one constant remains: indigenous languages and cultures have been historically subordinated to Spanish and to the cultural patterns and institutional norms associated with this language. To a large extent, this still holds true. Nonetheless, national legislation, in accordance with international legal instruments, such as the International Labour Organization Convention no. 169 on indigenous and tribal peoples (ILO 1989), of which Peru is a signatory, enshrines the linguistic rights of the Amerindian communities. Article 48 of the Constitution (Democratic Constituent Congress 1993) guarantees speakers of indigenous languages the right to an interpreter, ostensibly in recognition of their entitlement to use their native tongues in public and official settings. In 2003, a Languages Act (Congress of the Republic of Peru 2003) was passed. However, this legislation did not lead to an effective change in policy. The turning point in contemporary Peruvian language policy came in 2011, with the enactment of two pieces of legislation: a new Indigenous Languages Act (Congress of the Republic of Peru 2011b) and the Right to Prior Consultation Act (Congress of the Republic of Peru 2011a). It was the passing of these two Acts that led to the current processes for the implementation of the principles of language rights for indigenous peoples that will be discussed here.

This paper will outline the legal framework for the provision of interpreting services between Spanish and the indigenous languages of the country, before describing the State-sponsored interpreter training provision. It will conclude with an examination of the ensuing challenges that practitioners and institutions face.

Current Peruvian legal framework
on multilingualism and cultural diversity

The 2011 Indigenous Languages Act, to quote from its full title, "regulates the use, preservation, development, revitalization, promotion and diffusion of the indigenous languages of Peru." Its Article 4 states that every person has a right to the services of a "translator" for communication purposes in public service settings. Moreover, Article 20 stipulates that consultation and citizens' engagement processes pertaining to investment projects will be held in the indigenous language of the people(s) who inhabit the land where the projects are to be developed. As the language of the State is Spanish, this means, *de facto*, that the involvement of interpreters will be required in the consultations.

The Right to Prior Consultation Act focuses specifically on such consultation processes. According to this Act, the aim of the consultation is to reach an agreement between the State and the indigenous or native peoples by means of an "intercultural dialogue" that guarantees their inclusion in the decision-making processes of the State and the adoption of measures which respect their collective rights (article 3). Hence, this Act signaled a departure from the previous State practices as to the concession of rights to companies in indigenous peoples' territory: these concessions normally happened with very little (if any) consultation with the communities who were going to be affected. Article 16 of the Act guarantees the right to an interpreter in prior consultation processes, and, interestingly, stipulates that the interpreter must be trained in the specific subject matter of the consultation and registered by the governmental body specialized in indigenous affairs (De Pedro Ricoy et al. 2018b).

The passing of these two pieces of legislation, the Indigenous Languages Act and the Right to Prior Consultation Act, was momentous for two reasons. Firstly, the figure of the professional indigenous interpreter became publicly recognized for the first time in contemporary Peru. While bilingual indigenous people have acted as linguistic mediators between the native populations of the country and the Spanish-speaking administration since colonial times (De la Puente Luna 2014; Valdeón 2014), formal training, accreditation and registration of interpreters are new developments. As we will explain further on, the novelty of this situation has posed significant challenges, both to the State institutions and to the interpreters themselves. Secondly, the Acts demonstrate that access to justice is not restricted to informed participation in judicial processes, but that, rather, it also includes the right of the indigenous communities, historically marginalized, to be consulted on matters that affect them. Thus, the role of the indigenous legal interpreters is both to guarantee equality for individuals and to promote collective human rights.

As mentioned earlier, provision for the recognition of the language rights of indigenous peoples is laid down in domestic legislation (see Ruiz Molleda 2014) and also in international legal instruments, such as ILO Convention 169 and the 2007 UN Declaration on the Rights of Indigenous Peoples (UNDRIPS). However, its implementation failed to materialize, which had implications in terms of the recognition of cultural diversity within judicial processes. The question can be then asked as to what prompted the eventual enactment of the Indigenous Languages and Prior Consultation Acts in 2011 (Congress of the Republic of Peru 2011b; 2011a). The widely accepted answer is that they were triggered by "the Bagua massacre," commonly referred to in Spanish as "*el Baguazo*" (see Luna Amancio 2014). On 5 June 2009, violent clashes erupted between the local population and police forces that the State had sent to intervene in demonstrations by local mestizo and indigenous peoples close to the town of Bagua, in northeastern Amazonia. The clashes were the culmination of an escalation of tension and hostilities that arose because of an amendment to domestic legislation that aimed to simplify procedures for trading communal lands in Amazonian territories (see Cavero 2011), in a clear contravention of the rights of the indigenous communities. In the confrontation, hundreds were injured and the death toll was 33 – 10 civilians (indigenous and mestizo) and 23 police officers, according to official figures. Criminal charges were filed against 53 civilians, nine of them of Wampis ethnicity, 12 of Awajun ethnicity and one of Shawi ethnicity, as well as against 3 police officers.[2] Interpreters were brought in to serve during the high-profile trial of the indigenous defendants, as we shall describe below.

Also in 2011, the Peruvian Judiciary instigated the creation of a Working Group on Indigenous and Civil Justice (*Comisión de Trabajo sobre Justicia Indígena y Justicia de Paz*) with a view – to paraphrase from their documentation – to creating a roadmap to monitor the relationship of the State Judiciary with the indigenous justice systems, which are based on customary law, and making recommendations for the enhancement of

---

[2] See Molina (2016). The trial against the indigenous and mestizo defendants was closed on 22 September 2016. They were acquitted of all charges. The trial against the police officers has not started yet.

mutual understanding, cooperation and conflict resolution procedures.[3] This became the basis on which the Intercultural Justice system would be developed. According to the Inter-American Court of Human Rights (2005, p. 61), Intercultural Justice must give due consideration to the economic, social and cultural characteristics of indigenous people in any legal proceedings. Anthropologists may give expert evidence, and translators and interpreters must be involved to facilitate communication between the State institutions and the indigenous peoples. Three years later, as the Bagua trials were about to commence, Ruiz Molleda (2014), of the Legal Defence Institute (*Instituto de Defensa Legal*), quoting from proceedings of the International Court of Human Rights in relation to indigenous peoples and from the Peruvian State Constitution, asserted that "the Judiciary and the judges should not treat indigenous people in the same way as they would a citizen who is a member of the dominant culture."[4]

Institutional response

Thus, the development of the Intercultural Justice system, combined with the need for language brokering during the Bagua proceedings (which were eventually held between 2014 and 2016), brought into sharp focus the need to train and register translators and interpreters, as per the stipulations of the Indigenous Languages Act and the Right to Prior Consultation Act. This presented a notable challenge to the government, and, more specifically, to the Viceministry of Intercultural Affairs, instituted in 2010, which is the official body specialized in indigenous affairs. To address this challenge, the Ministry of Culture embarked on an ambitious interpreter training and qualification program with the ultimate aim of making provision for speakers

---

[3] "[D]icha Comisión de Trabajo tenía el propósito que sus integrantes desarrollen y monitoreen los componentes, acciones y tareas concretas de una hoja de ruta del Poder Judicial en su interrelación con la Justicia Indígena, tanto en lo referente al mutuo conocimiento de los sistemas de justicia a nivel sociológico y legal, a la coordinación entre sistemas de justicia y la resolución de conflictos entre ellos" ('The purpose of the said Working Group was for its members to develop and monitor the components, actions and specific tasks of a road map relevant to the relationship of the State Judiciary with the indigenous justice systems, relating to the mutual understanding of the justice systems on the sociological and legal levels, the coordination across justice systems and the resolution of conflicts arising between them') (Corte Superior de la República 2012). For an elaboration on these issues see the Peruvian Judiciary (2013).
[4] "[E]l Poder Judicial y los jueces 'no pueden dar a los miembros de los pueblos indígenas el mismo trato que le da [sic] a un ciudadano que participa de la cultura dominante." For a reflection on intercultural justice in Peru, see Peña Jumpa (2014).

of the 47 indigenous languages of the country. In 2012, the "Indigenous Languages Interpreter and Translator Training Course" (*Curso de Intérpretes y Traductores en Lenguas Indígenas*) was launched. An official Register of indigenous translators and/or interpreters was created in the same year and was granted legal status in 2016. Any public institution wishing to engage the services of indigenous translators and/or interpreters must now refer to this Register.

The basic training course is a three-week, non-language specific, intensive program underpinned by intercultural principles. Its curriculum covers legislation and rights, professional ethics, grammar, principles of translation and interpreting, and practical exercises in the latter. To date, there have been nine editions of the course, 307 translators and interpreters have qualified and 36 indigenous languages have been covered. Initially, the course prioritized training for participation in prior consultation processes. However, in response to the wider demands of the legislation, content related to public service interpreting and translation was introduced in the course from the sixth edition onwards. This diversification stemmed from the stipulations in the Indigenous Languages Act regarding access to public services in areas of the country where a given indigenous language predominates and responds to a real need, as, even where public servants are bilingual, the services are formally delivered in Spanish. Interestingly, the ethical and professional codes embedded in the training are those derived from the literature on community interpreting and are applied to language brokering in both public service settings and prior consultations, even though the latter is akin to business negotiations. In this regard, the lack of differentiation between the relevant codes of practice can impact on the rapport between the interlocutors and the interpreters, as we shall further mention below (see also De Pedro Ricoy et al. 2018b).

The basic course has been complemented by three-day specialized workshops, including ones dealing with prior consultation, which are institutionally run, and justice. These tend to focus on legal frameworks and the acquisition and clarification of relevant terminology. A monolingual (Spanish) glossary is compiled and updated by the Ministry of Culture on the basis of these workshops.

In addition, as a requirement for graduation from the course, the participants must complete a placement in a relevant public institution. These placements do not necessarily entail translation or interpreting activities, but they are a positive example of how the State has realized the value of continuous professional development and of situated learning. However, the process has not always been smooth, because of institutional and public perceptions, which we will deal with later.

The approach to the training provision can be justified by the diversity of the participants' profiles and the restricted resources available (human and otherwise), as well as by the need to cover as many indigenous languages as possible and achieve parity between the number of men and women represented, when the latter, in particular, are unlikely to be able to devote lengthy periods of time to the training. Having said that, it is undoubtedly a tall order to train translators and interpreters to a professional standard in three weeks, especially in the absence of qualified translation and/or interpreting trainers who are speakers of both Spanish and indigenous languages. It is also pertinent to note that, as our research revealed, a key motivation of the majority of the participants in the Course is not only to become accredited translators and/or interpreters but also, and importantly, to increase the visibility of their languages and cultures and promote the rights of their peoples (Andrade Ciudad et al. 2017a).

Challenges

Let us now consider the challenges that have emerged from this novel scenario, focusing on those that pertain specifically to interpreting. We will deal with procedural issues, management of the language transfer and institutional and public perceptions of the interpreters' practice, in that order.

Procedurally, the mechanisms for contracting interpreters are not yet well established.[5] For example, there was a delay to the opening of the Bagua trials because of some apparent confusion as to the provision of language mediation. No language assistance had been provided to the defendants beforehand,[6] and when the proceedings were due to start, as Ruiz Molleda (2014) reported, the Legal Defence Institute was informed that, as the Judiciary could not provide interpreting services, the Episcopal Commission on Social Action (CEAS) would supply its own. Thus, CEAS and the Legal Defence Institute started providing legal support to the indigenous leaders that were being prosecuted.

Eventually, the Ministry of Culture contacted two members of the first course cohort, a speaker of Wampis (henceforth, Interpreter 1) and a speaker of Awajun (henceforth, Interpreter 2), who agreed to provide their services.[7] In interviews that we conducted with them, they both stated that they took on

---

[5] A Protocol is being drafted by the Ministry of Culture.
[6] The absence of interpreting assistance in the stages of the proceedings prior to the trials is an irregularity that further underscores the fact that the provision of this kind of service is still very much in its infancy in Peru.
[7] The involvement of the interpreters in the Bagua trials has been the subject of media cover. See, e.g., Luna Amancio (2014) and ONAJUP (2014).

the job out of a sense of responsibility towards their peoples and to contribute to a satisfactory outcome for all the parties concerned. For example, Interpreter 2 recalled that he was criticized by other members of the Awajun people when he agreed to interpret at the proceedings, and explained his rationale in these words:

> I have not sold out; rather, this is an opportunity for expressing my feelings, what I want for myself and my country, and for my people as well. [...] Adopting a kind of mystical approach, I had to find a way of positioning myself for the common good (interview, Lima, 01/10/2015).[8]

Considering that both Interpreter 1 and Interpreter 2 are based in Lima and that they have jobs and family obligations, the weekly bus journey to Bagua, which takes over 20 hours each way, was a huge commitment, even more so because they started working without remuneration and, additionally, had to cover their own expenses as a result of the lack of procedural clarity mentioned earlier (see also Andrade Ciudad et al. 2017b). Interpreter 1 highlighted the stress that she was under throughout the initial stages of the assignment:

> I was informed a week before. A friend of mine told me that I was going to be the interpreter, and I said: "How come? Why? Why me?" [...] And I was phoned about, I don't know... three days before the trip, [and I was told] that I had to sign the contract. It was like that, total madness (interview, Lima, 10/03/2015).[9]

Interpreter 1 tellingly underscored issues of ethnic identification as one of the main tensions that arose during her first performances as judicial interpreter. Her testimony brings to the fore the conflicts that permeate neutrality and ethical protocols for interpreters of indigenous origin in postcolonial countries:

---

[8] "No me han comprado, sino que es una oportunidad para decir qué siento yo, qué deseo yo para mí y para mi país o para mi pueblo también. [...] Yo, haciendo una mística, tenía que ver la manera de ubicarme, para un bien común."

[9] "A mí me avisaron faltando una semana. Una amiga me dijo que yo iba a ser intérprete, y yo dije: Pero ¿cómo? ¿De dónde y por qué yo? [...] y me llamaron casi faltando no sé... tres días para el viaje, que tenía que firmar el contrato. Fue así, toda una locura total."

Although it is true that my closest relatives were not involved in the Bagua proceedings, the Bagua context is really relevant for us, it is very significant, and being there was like facing... facing again that movement, that situation, and two people were still remanded in custody, two Awajun, and they came to the hearing wearing handcuffs, and this was shocking for me [...]. During the training, we were always told about the need [for interpreters] to be neutral, that we had to interpret literally, that the matter under discussion, the stance held by either party are no concerns of ours, that our duty is to relay the message. I was clear about that but being there and watching all that was simply too much [...] because we arrived and we could not even greet them, because we were told [...] that we should not have any involvement with the defendants, in order to avoid misunderstandings on the part of the prosecutors or the judges (interview, Lima, 28/02/2015).[10]

The two interpreters also reported that, in spite of the fact that neither of them has a legal background, no briefing was initially provided and they were expected to "hit the ground running." Interpreter 1 told us:

In the first hearings, what I wanted to [know] was: how was I to act? How was I meant to deal with terms that I couldn't interpret on the spot? I had many doubts. I used to say to myself: "What do I do now?" I had a recurrent question: "How can I solve these doubts?" (interview, Lima, 28/02/2015).[11]

---

[10] "Si bien es cierto mis familiares directos no están involucrados en el caso de Bagua, el mismo contexto de Bagua es bastante fuerte para nosotros, es bastante significativo, y estar allí era como encontrarse, encontrarse con ese movimiento que hubo, con esa situación, y en ese momento todavía estaban con prisión preventiva dos personas, dos awajún, y venían enmarrocados a la audiencia y eso era chocante para mí [...]. En la capacitación siempre nos hablaron de que tenemos que ser neutrales, de que tenemos que interpretar literalmente, que no nos importa qué se está debatiendo, las posiciones que tienen ambos lados, nos importa transmitir el mensaje. Yo tenía claro eso, pero el estar en el momento y ver todo eso era bastante, [...] porque llegamos y ni siquiera podemos saludar porque nos habían dicho [...] que no teníamos que familiarizarnos con los acusados para poder evitar malas interpretaciones de los fiscales o de los jueces."
[11] "En las primeras audiencias yo lo que quería era [saber] cómo iba a actuar, cómo iba a enfrentar esos términos que en ese momento no podía darle interpretarlo, tenía muchas dudas, decía: '¿ahora qué hago?'. Estaba en esa constante pregunta. '¿Y cómo salgo de esas dudas?'"

The problems that, understandably, ensued were palliated when the proceedings were interrupted so that the National Office for Civil and Indigenous Justice (ONAJUP), in coordination with the Ministry of Culture, could brief them (ONAJUP 2014). This contributed to easing the working relations between the Court personnel and the interpreters.[12]

The Bagua proceedings were a landmark case in Peruvian legal history, because of the nature of the circumstances that led to them and, importantly, because indigenous interpreters trained and qualified by the State were employed for the first time in a Court of Law. What happens in other court cases is not as high profile or as widely reported, but it is reasonable to assume that issues of a similar kind are likely to arise and that the institutions should be working together to iron them out.

Moving on to matters that relate to the language transfer and the management thereof, we will firstly highlight linguistic and cultural asymmetries.

A clash of traditions and beliefs compounds the asymmetry of discursive and text-generic patterns between Spanish and indigenous languages. Spanish texts and discourses, when translated into the languages of peoples whose social structures and organization of legal matters are very different, remain alien, not because they cannot be expressed in those languages, but, rather, because they originated within a conceptual framework that the indigenous peoples do not necessarily share. An example of this can be found in the difficulty that translators had in expressing the concept of "rights" in the indigenous languages (for detail of this and other examples, see Howard et al. 2018). We will comment on two aspects related to these asymmetries.

Firstly, the emphasis that the State training course places on terminology, as evidenced in the focus on glossary construction,[13] risks creating a perception of lexical "deficiency" among the interpreters regarding the indigenous languages, which do not have "one-to-one equivalents" for technical or specialized terms that are, purportedly, common currency in the hegemonic language. In some ways, this echoes the discourse of churchmen of the colonial era, who complained of the inability of Quechua, for example, to express the tenets of the Christian faith (Mannheim 1991, p. 69). Whereas it is

---

[12] The problems that arose around the use of interpreters in the Bagua trial also led to the Indigenous Languages Division setting up a three-day intensive course in translation and interpreting in indigenous languages for intercultural justice, which took place in 2014. This model was expanded and the 9th edition of the three-week course (July 2016) was devoted entirely to this specialism.

[13] The Ministry of Culture coordinates the compilation of glossaries to provide explanatory equivalents that may assist the interpreters when performing their task.

true that language does not have a purely referential function, it is also true that alien or new concepts find their way into languages through the creation of "labels" that refer to them, through neologism, transliteration, calque or adaptation; and this indeed occurs (Howard et al. 2018; De Pedro Ricoy et al. 2018a). That is not the crux of the matter. The key consideration here should be that a person (or a linguistic community) may understand the denotation of a term, but not its connotation in the context of a hegemonic system whose legal parameters differ from their own. An example drawn from the charges against the indigenous people involved in the events in Bagua is illustrative of this: what happens if you have dispossessed a law-enforcing officer of his weapon when defending your rights? This is a criminal offense in the framework of a legal system, derived from Roman Law, that is alien to you. What happens if you do not consider the act to be a criminal offense? Should the principle that *ignoratia juris non excusat* apply?

Secondly, the emphasis on terminology and phraseology detracts from the attention that should be paid to the asymmetries in discursive patterns and practices. Instruction, exposition and argumentation are textually instantiated according to language-specific rules and norms. Therefore, it seems reasonable to assume that, in the course of lengthy criminal proceedings conducted across languages that reflect very different world views, such asymmetries are likely to cause misunderstandings and even a potential breakdown in communication. Interpreter 2 elaborated:

> It is a very complex situation, because we are facing two different realities. [...]. Here, each crime is punished according to its degree of severity, but adapting this to my reality posed great complexity. So, what we did, or what I did, was to look for a word that could be a close translation, because in our language there are no words for those crimes. For example, "rape". [...] But I also had in mind that those two worlds were coming face to face, meeting each other for the first time. [...] "Culpable homicide", for example, that doesn't exist, and we asked ourselves: "What should I say?". "Culpable homicide," "dispossessing

an officer of a firearm" [...]. And also "public obstruction" (interview, Lima, 01/10/2015).[14]

Another aspect that merits consideration is the hegemonic place of Spanish in Peru. The assumption that it works well as a *lingua franca* in public service settings is potentially misleading, in that it can be used to argue that the use of interpreters is unnecessary. The view that interpretation is required only for indigenous people who are monolingual prevails in the public arena, although monolingualism is no longer the norm among indigenous populations.

In relation to this, Interpreter 1 recounted that, even though she perceived an "evolution" among the judges in the Bagua trial regarding intercultural matters, at the beginning they adopted an aggressive stance towards the defendants, pointing to their bilingualism and their knowledge of Spanish as evidence of the fact that they did not need an interpreter at all:

> They were cruel towards the defendants. They told them: "Hey, be honest: if you speak Spanish, if you understand it, just say that you will testify in Spanish, and those who don't understand it at all, may testify in their language." Those were the rules (interview, Lima, 10/03/2015).[15]

Although most indigenous people will have some knowledge of Spanish, this does not mean that they are proficient enough in that language to enter into a meaningful (and often essential) dialogue with the institutions.[16] The situation is aggravated by the historical discrimination that the indigenous

---

[14] "Es complicado, porque son dos realidades [...]. Aquí se castiga el nivel o el grado del caso, pero adaptar prácticamente a mi realidad era complicado. Entonces, lo que hicimos o lo que hice es buscar un término más o menos que se aproxima a la traducción, porque en el idioma no hay palabras para esos casos. Por ejemplo, 'violaciones'. [...] Pero también consciente de que esos dos mundos se encuentran recién, se conocen recién por primera vez. [...] 'Homicidio culposo' por ejemplo, que no existe, y nos preguntábamos: '¿Qué digo?' 'Homicidio culposo', 'arrebato de armas' [...]. Y después 'obstrucción de vía pública.'"

[15] "Eran crueles con los acusados. Les decían así: 'Oye, sean sinceros: si hablan el castellano, si entienden, digan que van a declarar en castellano, y las personas que no entienden en absoluto, que declaren en su idioma'. Eran esas reglas."

[16] This is also documented for other geographical-cultural contexts. For instance, Cooke (2002) reported the case of Australian Aboriginal defendants whose level of English competency was shown to be inadequate to deal with the legal proceedings with which they were confronted. This inadequacy could go unrecognized by the authorities, potentially leading to miscarriages of justice.

peoples of Peru have suffered, which in some cases results in a reluctance to use their own languages in official or professional settings, for fear of being considered "inferior." Additionally, some languages have very few speakers remaining, and a wholesale shift to Spanish has taken place in some communities, leading speakers to question the need for interpreting when dealing with the institutions in, for instance, prior consultation processes. Yet again, as we mentioned in the introduction of this chapter, speakers of non-standard Spanish may also meet discrimination on linguistic grounds.

We will now focus on the challenges that concern the professional practice of the interpreters and how public service providers and civil society perceive it.

The lack of familiarity with the figure of the indigenous interpreter in contemporary Peru can lead to misconceptions as to their role and what interpreting entails. The indigenous beneficiaries of interpreting services are not necessarily more familiar with the role of the interpreter than the rest of society. As mentioned previously, some of them are bilingual and can, therefore, monitor and evaluate the interpreter's performance in both languages. This may lead to a lack of trust and to erroneous expectations. For example, the Wampis interpreter in the Bagua proceedings related how she was criticized for seeking clarification "too often" as if omitting or distorting information was preferable:

> And then, when the day of the hearing arrived, I had doubts [...]. So, I put questions to the prosecutor, to, please, provide clarification of such and such a term, and this went on for almost the whole hearing in which the charges were read. It was plain to see that I was being criticized. I don't know if some of the ones that were published, the articles that appeared in the press [saying] that we lacked the required competence [...], and the judiciary was also heavily criticized, the ministries were heavily criticized, so we also ended up on the receiving end (interview, Lima, 28/02/2015).[17]

Furthermore, press coverage at the time criticized the interpretation for not complying with international standards, in that it was not performed in the

---

[17] "Entonces, cuando llegó el día de la audiencia, yo en ese momento tenía dudas [...]. Entonces, yo lancé las preguntas al fiscal que me aclarara, por favor, tal término, tal término, y así, casi toda la audiencia cuando se leyó la acusación fiscal. Y allí pudieron notar también que me criticaron. No sé si algunos que salieron, las notas que salió en los medios que no estábamos preparados [...] y criticaron mucho al Poder Judicial, criticaron mucho a los ministerios y, pues, a nosotros también nos cayó."

simultaneous mode (Wiesse and Saravia 2014). In fact, there are no international standards that stipulate that interpreting should be conducted simultaneously in court proceedings and, moreover, this does not occur routinely. More importantly, it would have been impossible to provide simultaneous interpreting in Bagua, due to the lack of technical equipment and booths in the Court. Such ill-founded criticism is bound to have a detrimental effect on the interpreters' morale and can also misguide public opinion as to the value of their role.

Another consequence of the lack of familiarity with the remit of the indigenous interpreters and the limits of their role is the potential for mistrust to be generated across the triadic relation between the judiciary, the interpreter and the indigenous beneficiaries of the interpretation. During the State-sponsored training, the neutrality of the interpreter is highlighted as "a must," and we have evidence that the trainees engage well with the principle: they often describe themselves as "conduits" for the voices of others and aspire to be "invisible." However, the presumption of neutrality can be challenged by both sets of interlocutors involved in the mediated exchange: the representatives of the legal institutions may feel that the interpreter aligns himself or herself with his or her own people and, therefore, manipulates the information; on the other hand, the indigenous communities may believe that an interpreter trained and employed by the State is betraying his or her people by serving its interests.

In conversation with us, employees of the Ministry of Culture provided examples of how this tension can manifest itself: for example, one interpreter demanded a very high fee because he considered that he was "harming his people" in his mediation role during a prior consultation process, and another expressed his frustration at not being allowed to provide advice to his community and to represent it in the way he thought best in front of the State representatives, for which reason he had to be replaced. Issues of (mis)trust also lead to communicative situations in which two interpreters are present in prior consultation processes: one trained and employed by the Ministry and another, unqualified and untrained (although often with informal experience of the task), appointed by the community. Although the presence of two or more interpreters is not uncommon in business negotiations, this situation has led to a perceived hierarchy of interpreters when the State trained and "local" interpreters find themselves sharing the same space, and also to problems related to the construction of trust. There is awareness of this issue on the part of both trainers and trainees, and efforts are made to resolve it (De Pedro Ricoy et al. 2018b).

Beyond State provision: grassroots initiatives

While our research under the aegis of the AHRC project mainly focused on State training of indigenous interpreters and translators, as discussed so far, our collaboration with the NGO *Servicios Educativos Rurales* (*SER*) as project partners (see note 1) also brought to light the practice of community interpreting conducted in other arenas, beyond the orbit of the formal training program. As a result of her work with indigenous women's organizations in the southern Peruvian Andes, Raquel Reynoso (President of *SER*) brought to our attention the existence of a figure that she named the *traductora social* ("social interpreter," Reynoso 2016).

The *traductoras sociales* are female speakers of both Spanish and Quechua or Aymara who help out on an *ad hoc* basis in public service settings or formal meetings involving indigenous women who need interpreting support. As well as providing a service of cultural and linguistic mediation, they also work with rural women, whose right to participate in the governance of their communities and the management of the communal land and resources is rarely recognized, by raising awareness and providing relevant training. Their involvement in language-brokering is a bottom-up initiative motivated by the desire to serve the interest of minoritized groups that has arisen quite independently of the State.

In August 2016, *SER* informed us of a new development whereby the social interpreters have been called upon to serve in the context of the National Commission to register the testimonies of the women who were the victims of a compulsory sterilization program over the 1996-2000 period. The government in power in 1995 introduced an amendment to the General Population Law to include sterilization as a contraceptive method, on the principle that lower birth rates would drive down poverty. One year later, the Reproductive Health and Family Planning Program (*Programa de Salud Reproductiva y Planificación Familiar*) was launched. Nearly 315,000 women, most of them indigenous, were subjected to sterilization under this program. According to the Latin American and Caribbean Commission for the Rights of Women (CLADEM), only 10% gave their consent to the procedure (Lizarzaburu 2015).

The first death came in 1996 and from then onwards a high number of illegal procedures started to be reported. The Peruvian Office of the Ombudsman (*Defensoría del Pueblo*) published three reports that presented findings regarding the absence of guarantees for informed consent, the undue pressure that women were put under, and the lack of aftercare. Two of the key recommendations were that women who were forcibly sterilized should receive compensation and that all cases of compulsory sterilization should be investigated.

A Register of Victims of Forced Sterilization (*Registro de Víctimas de Esterilizaciones Forzadas - REVIESFO*) is currently being compiled by the Ministry of Justice and Human Rights, with a view to seeking legal redress for the victims. As mentioned, most of the latter are women speakers of indigenous languages, from poor, rural backgrounds and have low levels of formal education. Interpreters were recruited to assist with the gathering of testimonies that will be the basis for a record of the cases. As we learned from a speaker at an event we held in Ayacucho in August 2016, who works alongside the REVIESFO Commission, only male interpreters had been recruited, due to non-availability of accredited female ones. This, inevitably, had consequences for the effectiveness of an interpretation process that involved women's testimonies of such an intimate nature. As an upshot of the event, as *SER* subsequently reported to us, the social interpreters with whom they have hitherto been working in other contexts have now been recruited to support the work of the *REVIESFO* Commission.

This is an example of how, where adequate official provision is not readily at hand, initiatives may be taken at the grassroots, motivated by the need to serve the interests of minoritized and vulnerable groups. The topic merits further research to see how, potentially, the grassroots experience of the social interpreters might come to inform and articulate with State policy and provision.

Concluding remarks

Much ground has been covered and considerable progress has been made in a relatively short period of time in Peru as to the provision of interpreting services between Spanish and the indigenous languages of the country. The processes that the State has put in place could be consolidated in a number of ways, and these concluding remarks are intended by way of suggestions.[18]

Generic interpreter training could be followed by further specialization and continuous professional development to guarantee adequate service levels. As for the management of the interpreters' involvement in guaranteeing access to justice, in the case of prosecutions, the Judiciary could ensure that interpreters are involved at all the stages (police interviews, liaison with lawyers, statement-giving, statement-signing, etc.), and not only in court proceedings. Prior consultation provides a good model for this, as the

---

[18] These suggestions arise from our observations during the period of the research project; new developments in these directions may have unfolded since that period.

interpreters already participate in all the relevant stages of the process. In addition, sound protocols for the employment of interpreters (including a fee structure) could be developed, as well as a specific code of practice for indigenous interpreters that is relevant to the socio-political backdrop to their role. Finally, more could be done institutionally to redress the gender imbalance and create incentives for indigenous women to train and qualify as interpreters.

More widely, awareness of the role of indigenous interpreters could be further raised among the users of their services and civil society alike. It is crucial that the scope of both the interpreters' role and its boundaries be socialized in a country that is still characterized by acute inequality and discrimination against indigenous peoples. It is also essential to address the specifics of a situation where a level of bilingualism is presumed of indigenous people, where linguistic and cultural asymmetries impinge greatly on the interpreting process, and where the scales of power tip manifestly in favor of one linguistic community for historical reasons. Otherwise, there is a risk that indigenous interpreters may be considered, at worst, redundant (as a representative of the Ministry of Energy and Mines said after a training workshop for a prior consultation process, "using Spanish, we will always more or less understand one another") and, at best, an expensive add-on motivated by political correctness. The role of the indigenous interpreters is a cornerstone in the safeguard of the human rights of Peruvian minoritized communities and their access to justice, and it needs to be recognized as such.

References

Andrade Ciudad, Luis, Rosaleen Howard & Raquel De Pedro Ricoy, 2017a. Activismo, derechos lingüísticos e ideologías: la traducción e interpretación en lenguas originarias en el Perú. *Indiana*, 32(2).

——, 2017b. Traduciendo culturas en el Perú: los derechos lingüísticos en la práctica. *In:* Marleen Haboud & Azuccna Palacios, eds. *Lenguas en contacto: Desafíos en la diversidad.* Quito: Pontificia Universidad Católica de Ecuador.

Cavero, Omar, 2011. Después del Baguazo: informes, diálogo y debates. *Cuadernos de Trabajo del Departamento de Ciencias Sociales de la PUCP: Serie Justicia y Conflictos*, 13(1), 6-72. Online: http://cisepa.pucp.edu.pe/wp-content/uploads/2016/07/baguazo_cavero.pdf.

Cerrón-Palomino, Rodolfo, 2003. *Castellano Andino: Aspectos Sociolingüísticos, Pedagógicos y Gramaticales.* Lima: PUCP/GTZ.

Congress of the Republic of Peru, 2003. Ley de reconocimiento, preservación, fomento y difusión de las lenguas aborígenes, No. 28106, Lima, El Peruano. Online:

https://centroderecursos.cultura.pe/sites/default/files/rb/pdf/Ley29735Le ydelenguas2011.pdf.

———, 2011a. Ley del derecho a la consulta previa a los pueblos indígenas u originarios, No. 29785, Lima, El Peruano. Online: http://www.ilo.org/dyn/natlex/docs/ELECTRONIC/88881/101786/F114786 124/PER88881.pdf.

———, 2011b. Ley que regula el uso, preservación, desarollo, recuperación, fomento y difusión de las lenguas originarias del Perú, Lima, El Peruano. Online: https://centroderecursos.cultura.pe/sites/default/files/rb/pdf/Ley29735Le ydelenguas2011.pdf.

Cooke, Michael, 2002. *Indigenous Interpreting Issues for Courts*. Carlton, Victoria: Australian Institute of Judicial Administration.

Corte Superior de la República, 2012. Resolución Administrativa N° 499-2012-P-PJ. Online: http://www.onajup.gob.pe/wp-content/uploads/2014/03/Hoja-de-Ruta-de-la-Justicia-Intercultural-2012.pdf.

Democratic Constituent Congress, 1993. Constitución Política del Perú, Lima. Online: http://www2.congreso.gob.pe/sicr/RelatAgenda/constitucion.nsf/constituc ion.

Escobar, Alberto 1978. *Variaciones sociolingüísticas del castellano en el Perú*. Lima: Instituto de Estudios Peruanos.

De los Heros, Susana, 1999. Prestigio abierto y encubierto: las actitudes hacia las variantes del castellano hablado en el Perú. *Revista de Humanidades*, 6, 13-44.

Howard, Rosaleen, Luis Andrade Ciudad & Raquel de Pedro Ricoy, 2018. Translating Rights: the Peruvian Languages Act in Quechua and Aymara. *Amerindia*, 40, 219-245.

ILO (International Labour Organization), 1989. Indigenous and Tribal Peoples Convention, 76th ILC session, No. 169, Geneva.

Inter-American Court of Human Rights, 2005. Caso Comunidad Indígena Yakye Axa Vs. Paraguay, San José. Online: http://www.corteidh.or.cr/docs/casos/articulos/seriec_125_esp.pdf.

Lizarzaburu, Javier, 2015. Forced sterilisation haunts Peruvian women decades on, *BBC*, Lima. Online: http://www.bbc.co.uk/news/world-latin-america-34855804.

Luna Amancio, Nelly, 2014. El "Baguazo": la complejidad de un juicio en el que los cargos no tienen traducción, *BBC*, Lima. Online: http://www.bbc.com/mundo/noticias/2014/06/140605_peru_baguazo_inte rprete_en.

Mannheim, Bruce, 1991. *The Language of the Inka since the European Invasion*. Austin: University of Texas Press.

Molina, Natalia, 2016. Baguazo: comenzó lectura de sentencia de caso Curva del Diablo, *El Comercio*, Lima: Grupo de Diarios América. Online: http://elcomercio.pe/peru/baguazo-comenzo-lectura-sentencia-caso-curva-diablo-261109.

ONAJUP (Oficina Nacional de Justicia de Paz y de Justicia Indígena), 2014. *La ONAJUP capacitó a intérpretes oficiales del caso de Bagua*, Lima: ONAJUP. Online: http://www.onajup.gob.pe/la-onajup-capacito-interpretes-oficiales-del-caso-de-bagua/.

De Pedro Ricoy, Raquel, Rosaleen Howard & Luis Andrade Ciudad, 2018a. Translators' Perspectives: The construction of the Peruvian Indigenous Languages Act in indigenous languages. *Meta*, 63(2), 159-176.

———, 2018b. Walking the Tightrope: The role of Peruvian indigenous interpreters in Prior Consultation processes. *Target*.

Peña Jumpa, Antonio, 2014. *Sin una justicia intercultural no nos podemos integrar como país*, Lima: SERVINDI. Online: https://www.servindi.org/actualidad/115088.

the Peruvian Judiciary, 2013. *Protocolo de Coordinación entre Sistemas de Justicia Protocolo de Actuación en Procesos Judiciales que Involucren a Comuneros y Ronderos*, Madrid: Eurosocial. Online: http://sia.eurosocial-ii.eu/files/docs/1396262790-Protocolo_Peru_Actuacion_procesos judiciales_comuneros_ronderos.pdf.

De la Puente Luna, José Carlos, 2014. The Many Tongues of the King: Indigenous Language Interpreters and the Making of the Spanish Empire. *Colonial Latin American Review*, 23(2), 143-170.

Reynoso, Raquel, 2016. Traductoras y programas de capacitación a líderes y lideresas. Una experiencia desde la sociedad civil, in *International Symposium "Traducción e interpretación en las lenguas originarias del Perú."* Lima: Universidad Peruana de Ciencias Aplicadas. Online: http://research.ncl.ac.uk/translatingculturesperu/.

Ruiz Molleda, Juan Carlos, 2014. *Justicia debe considerar 'diferencia cultural' al imputar responsabilidad penal*, Lima: SERVINDI. Online: https://www.servindi.org/actualidad/106415.

Sichra, Inge, 2009. *The Sociolinguistic Atlas of Indigenous Peoples in Latin America: a tool for planning regarding education and indigenous peoples*. London: MRG International.

Valdeón, Roberto A., 2014. *Translation and the Spanish Empire in the Americas*. Amsterdam, Philadelphia: John Benjamins Publishing Company.

Wiesse, Patricia & Gerardo Saravia, 2014. El banquillo de los inocentes (y el solaz de los culpables). *Revista Ideele*, 239. Online: http://revistaideele.com/ideele/content/el-banquillo-de-los-inocentes-y-el-solaz-de-los-culpables.

Zavala, Virginia & Gavina Córdova, 2010. *Decir y callar. Lenguaje, equidad y poder en la Universidad peruana*. Lima: Fondo Editorial de la Pontificia Universidad Católica del Perú.

Chapter 7

Translation and interpreting policies in China:
Ethnic linguistic minorities in the judicial system

Shuang Li

In China, ethnic linguistic minorities' rights to translation services in judicial proceedings are explicitly guaranteed by the Constitution of the People's Republic of China (PRC) and other national laws. However, despite the increasingly important role of translating and interpreting, previous studies have shown that discrepancies exist between the legislation governing the use of translation and/or interpreting and what has come true in reality. To shed light on the reasons behind such mismatch, this chapter intends to first discuss the interactions among the three components of translation policy (i.e. translation management, translation practices and translation beliefs) and then trace the social, political and historical factors that have forged current translation policies and their possibilities.

Bridging the language gap: equal access to justice

In multi-ethnic China, the Han people, the dominant nationality in China, constitute about 91.51 percent of the country's total population of approximately 1.34 billion, whereas the other 55 ethnic minority groups account for around 8.49 percent of the total population (National Bureau of Statistics of China 2013). More than 80 indigenous languages and more than 30 written scripts are currently used in China (Ministry of Education of the People's Republic of China 2013).

In such a multilingual context with pronounced linguistic and cultural differences, language work is an indispensable part in promoting participatory citizenship in public affairs and fostering social integration. To bridge the gap among different language groups, the government has promoted Mandarin Chinese as the shared, national and official lingua franca throughout the whole nation. The amended 1982 Constitution of the PRC for the first time clearly distinguished Mandarin Chinese, the nationally promoted language, from those non-nationally promoted languages (The National People's Congress NPC 1982, article 19; Zhou 2004b). In 2000, the National People's Congress Standing Committee (NPCSC) enacted the Law of the National Commonly Used Language and Script of the PRC, which identifies 'the national standard spoken and written language' as Mandarin Chinese and the standardized Chinese characters (NPCSC 2000, articles 2 and 3). As a result of such a language policy, Mandarin Chinese and the standardized Chinese characters play a predominant role in government administration, the legal domain, education, the media and the business industries, as well as other major public sectors of society across the whole country.

However, it should be noted that according to the MOE, a third of China's population are still unable to speak Mandarin Chinese and that many Mandarin-speakers only have a limited proficiency in it (Liu and Wu 2013). In fact, in recent decades, China's marked increase in urbanization and population mobility across language borders has complicated local administration and has challenged policy makers to ensure equal access to public services for all Chinese citizens. And at the same time, people who only have a partial or non-existent mastery of the spoken Mandarin Chinese and standard Chinese characters are also confronted with the challenge of adapting themselves to a new linguistic environment when they cross language borders within the country. For example, the past few years have witnessed an increase in the number of ethnic migrant workers from rural areas to urban areas, hoping to improve their social and economic wellbeing. However, many of them have encountered linguistic difficulties, which remain one of the barriers to their fuller integration into the urban society (Guo and Zhang 2010).

Striving to achieve a "relationship of equality, unity and mutual assistance among all of China's ethnic groups" is a moral imperative grounded in the Constitution of the PRC (NPC 1982, article 4). When it comes to language use, the PRC Constitution stipulates that all ethnic groups enjoy constitutionally equal status and have the right to use and develop their languages in the political, judicial, and social realms of their lives (NPC 1982, article 4, 121 and 134). One of the prominent public policy issues that cannot be ignored is the removal of linguistic barriers in the courts. Indeed, judicial settings serve as an essential domain in safeguarding citizens' fundamental rights (González Núñez 2016, p. 197). Furthermore, access to the judicial system is a precondition for ensuring justice and equality. As a growing number of legal cases involve different ethnic groups, China's policy makers have become increasingly aware of the barriers that language differences have produced in the administration of justice. Therefore, the policy makers have adopted language and translation policies to provide language services in the justice system for ethnic linguistic minorities to guarantee true and equal access to the court. Among the language services, translating and interpreting are often involved. As a matter of fact, ethnic linguistic minorities' rights to translation services in judicial proceedings are explicitly guaranteed by the Constitution of the PRC, the Criminal Procedure Law of the PRC (NPC 1979a, article 9), the Administrative Litigation Law of the PRC (NPC 1989, article 9), the Civil Procedure Law of the PRC (NPC 1991, article 11), the Organic Law of the People's Courts of the PRC (NPC 1979b, article 6) and the Law of the PRC on Regional National Autonomy (NPC 1984, article 47).

However, despite the increasingly important role of translating and interpreting, previous studies have shown that discrepancies exist between the legislation governing the use of translation and/or interpreting and what has come true in reality (Li 2017; Li et al. 2017). Existing problems in translation practices cannot be simply resolved by the authorities' linear interventions. To explain the reasons behind this and to explore potential solutions to improve this situation, this chapter intends to first discuss the interactions among the three components of translation policy[1] (i.e. translation management, translation practices and translation beliefs) and then trace the social, political and historical factors that have forged current translation policies and their possibilities.

---

[1] According to Meylaerts (2011) and González Núñez (2013), translation policy encompasses translation management, translation practices and translation beliefs. Translation management refers to "the decisions regarding translation made by people in authority to decide a domain's use or non-use of translation" (González Núñez 2016, p. 54). Translation management can be considered as explicit policy and often takes the form of a series of codified or written documents, ranging from national legislation to a local institution's in-house guidelines (ibid). Translation practices refer to actual translation activities in a given community (ibid). It should be noted that what has happened in reality is not always explicitly mandated through translation management, and vice versa. Translation beliefs are the values assigned by members of a community to translation. This involves "issues such as what the value is or is not of offering translation in certain contexts for certain groups or to achieve certain ends" (González Núñez 2016, p. 55). For a detailed discussion about defining translation policy, see González Núñez (2016: 50-56).

Translating and interpreting for ethnic linguistic minorities in China: a policy study in judicial settings

This study employs a descriptive-explanatory approach within a theoretical framework shaped by a three-level definition of translation policy and complexity theory. The three-level definition of translation policy proposed by Meylaerts (2011) and González Núñez (2013) is methodologically useful in that it enables researchers to understand not only explicit legislation and regulations but also their real consequences as well as the implicit intended purposes of certain legislation. Therefore, this study leans on their understanding of translation policy. However, we should be aware of the danger of focusing on the search for the three simple units of translation policy from a fragmentary approach. Translation policy is not simply the sum of its constituent parts and it is much more complex than we could imagine. Even if we may be able to thoroughly describe each component of translation policy separately, we would still be confronted with questions concerning occasional contradictions between translation management, translation practices and translation beliefs, unsatisfactory and unequal implementation of legislation on language issues, and uncertain and unpredictable properties of translation policy (cf. Meylaerts 2017).

Increasing recognition of the complex nature of policy processes has prompted many scholars from policy-related fields (e.g. Cairney 2012; Bastardas-Boada 2013; Meylaerts 2017; among others) to reconsider the methodologies for studying public policy, language and translation policy and planning. There is a general recognition among them that it is high time that we transcended the traditional reductionist approach by adopting a more integrated and comprehensive approach resorting to the concepts and insights of complexity theory, which considers policy as a complex system in which a network of interdependent elements "interact with each other, share information and combine to produce systemic behaviour" (Cairney 2012). Complexity theory also shows an interest in "how wholes constrain parts" (Van Kooten Niekerk and Buhl 2004, p. 4). According to Jan Smuts (1926; cited in Marais 2015, p. 19), "evolution is driven by the needs or requirements of a whole, not the parts, and that one thus has to focus your interest on understanding wholes." Therefore, a complexity approach takes account of both "how parts relate to one another to create wholes" and "how wholes constrain parts." By drawing upon this holistic view on policy system, this translation policy study hopes to avoid limiting itself to one specific component of translation policy. Instead, it will concentrate on the interactions among the constituent parts of translation policy as well as the interrelationship between the parts and the whole.

The data presented are drawn from official legislation, directives and regulations, previous empirical studies, legal journals and news reports. Due to the large number of ethnic minority groups distributed all over China, it is impossible to cover every ethnic minority group and every minority language in this single study. Nonetheless, this study intends to explore how regions with different ethnic compositions handle specific challenges caused by multilingualism, as previous studies show that language and translation practices vary depending on the relative population concentration of a minority group (Zhou 2004b; Li et al. 2017). Therefore, the case studies selected in this research will involve not only autonomous regions largely inhabited by one specific ethnic minority group but also autonomous regions inhabited by a variety of ethnic minority groups as well as areas mainly inhabited by Han Chinese.

Court translation and interpreting

Several national laws explicitly mandate the use of minority languages in courts proceedings when the minority languages are commonly used in local regions largely inhabited by a specific ethnic minority group or by a variety of ethnic minority groups. For example, the PRC's current Constitution (NPC 1982, article 134) states that:

> Citizens of all China's nationalities have the right to use their native spoken and written languages in court proceedings. The people's courts and people's procuratorates should provide translation for any party to the court proceedings who is not familiar with the spoken or written languages commonly used in the locality.
>
> In an area where people of a minority nationality live in a concentrated community or where a number of nationalities live together, court hearings should be conducted in the language or languages commonly used in the locality; indictments, judgments, notices and other documents should be written, according to actual needs, in the language or languages commonly used in the locality (NPC 1982, article 134; official translation in a booklet published by Foreign Language Press, 1999).

According to this article, China's translation management in the judiciary explicitly points out the obligations imposed on people's courts and people's procuratorates to provide translation and interpreting services for any Chinese citizen with limited proficiency in the spoken or written languages commonly used in the locality. Such state obligations can also be found in other national laws, such as the Criminal Procedure Law of the PRC (NPC

1979a, article 9), the Administrative Litigation Law of the PRC (NPC 1989, article 9), the Civil Procedure Law of the PRC (NPC 1991, article 11), the Organic Law of the People's Courts of the PRC (NPC 1979b, article 6) and the Law of the PRC on Regional National Autonomy (NPC 1984, article 47). It can be discerned that court translation and interpreting are valued by the government as a key way to guarantee all Chinese citizens' linguistic rights and ensure access to justice for all.

Such translation management, which is featured by institutional multilingualism as an institutional support for ethnic linguistic minorities (Li 2017), has a certain top-down influence on translation practices and translation beliefs. Translation management plays a vital role in raising awareness of the pivotal role of professional court translation and interpreting in bridging language gaps between the courts and citizens who are unable to communicate in the language of the court. For instance, according to a governmental website (Supreme People's Court of the People's Republic of China 2017) with full videos of trials throughout the country, when defendants in criminal trials have limited proficiency in Mandarin Chinese, some judges, by stating relevant articles of current laws, inform the defendants of their rights to use their mother tongues and to have court interpreters made available for them. This aims to ensure the fair administration of justice and to enable meaningful communication that allows ethnic linguistic minorities to exercise their inalienable constitutional rights. And accordingly, some local courts and procuratorates have adopted practical measures to guarantee the quality of legal translation and interpreting services. Some new translation practices have emerged locally for practical needs. The People's Court of Wuhou District in Chengdu[2] can serve as an example. When the People's Court of Wuhou District in Chengdu deals with criminal cases involving Tibetan citizens, it provides the defendant with two or three interpreters (Wang 2014), since the three oral dialects of Tibetan language are, to a great extent, mutually unintelligible (Zhou 2004a, p. 225). The interpreters interact with the defendant before a trial and the one whose dialect is the closest to the defendant's dialect will take a leading part in interpreting in court (ibid). Another example is the People's Procuratorate of Hanyuan county[3] in Ya'an city in Sichuan province. Hanyuan People's

---

[2] Chengdu, as one of the most important metropolis in the southwest of China, is mainly inhabited by Han Chinese, and at the same time it also has inhabitants from other 55 ethnic minority groups.

[3] Inhabitants in Hanyuan county are from Han, Yi, Tibetan, Hui and other 13 ethnic groups. The Han people account for 90 percent of the local population, while ethnic minority groups constitute 10 percent.

Procuratorate realized the shortcomings in its previous practices of employing *ad hoc* translators and interpreters (Chen and Liu 2015). To standardize translation and interpreting in criminal proceedings, Hanyuan People's Procuratorate cooperated with the Bureau of the Ethnic and Religious Affairs of Hanyuan County to draw up guidelines on the qualifications, rights, and duties of translators and interpreters (ibid).

However, this does not mean that what has been stipulated by law never fails to come true in reality. It is noteworthy that translation practices and translation beliefs can vary widely from place to place and from person to person, even when translation management is the same at national level. In other words, even though translation practices and translation beliefs accept influences from translation management, they may also resist the impact of translation management and may consequently result in different negative or positive effects of translation policy. For instance, despite the fact that some policy makers, court administrators and legal professionals (e.g. A'nisha 2009; Cairang 2014; Wang 2014) have recognized the important role played by court translation and interpreting in removing linguistic barriers to justice, there is still a lack of consensus among individuals about who to translate or interpret, when to translate or interpret and how to translate or interpret in judicial proceedings (cf. Shi and Zhao 2012; Lu 2015). This is largely attributed to one of the major limitations of current translation management, that is, the lack of systematic legislation on translating or interpreting for ethnic linguistic minorities in judicial proceedings. All of the existing articles are scattered in different laws and are too abstract to execute (A'nisha 2009).

Admittedly, the Civil Procedure Law of the PRC and the Administrative Litigation Law of the PRC include articles with regard to the disqualification of a court translator or interpreter. Specifically, court translators and interpreters are supposed to voluntarily disqualify themselves when they deem that they have an interest in the case, which may affect the impartial trial of the case (NPC 1989, article 55; 1991, article 44). A party to a case is entitled to request disqualification of a translator or an interpreter, when the party deems that the translator or the interpreter has an interest in the case, which may affect the fair administration of justice (ibid). However, these articles do not include insufficient language, translation, interpreting or other professional skills as possibilities of disqualifying a court translator or interpreter. All in all, the instructions on court translation and interpreting given in current laws remain very general without systematic and standard operating rules regulating the production of certified translations or interpreting, the qualifications of court translators and interpreters, the training and employment of certified court translators and interpreters and so on. It is also noteworthy that existing legal provisions are not devoted to translation and interpreting in a separate way, which indicates the lack of governmental awareness of differentiating between written translation and oral interpreting.

Another problem is a shortage of explicit legislative enactments with regard to the rights and duties of translators and interpreters. Only the Criminal Law of the PRC includes a relevant article:

> If, in criminal proceedings, a witness, expert witness, recorder or interpreter intentionally gives false testimony or makes a false expert evaluation, record or translation concerning the circumstances that have an important bearing on a case, in order to frame another person or conceal criminal evidence, he shall be sentenced to fixed-term imprisonment of not more than three years or criminal detention; if the circumstances are serious, he shall be sentenced to fixed-term imprisonment of not less than three years but not more than seven years. (NPC 1997, article 305)

This is an important article, yet when it comes to the exact duties of translators and interpreters in criminal proceedings, it remains silent. This article only takes account of false translation but does not address unintentional mistakes or inappropriate translation that may result in delays in the commencement of proceedings, delays in commencing an arbitration and even miscarriages of justice.

Influenced by the limitations of translation management mentioned above, there is also a persistent belief among some courts and even some translators or interpreters that any bilingual individual can perform court translation and interpreting (Wang 2014). As a consequence, it is common that some local courts are not equipped with full-time professional legal translators or interpreters (Wu 2009; Wang 2014). In many cases, bilingual and multilingual individuals, including university professors, university students, police officers, lawyers, or any other alleged bilingual person, are called on to offer translation or interpreting services, even though they have not been formally trained to be a legal translator or an interpreter. For instance, bilingual judges, collegial panels, legal-aid attorneys, agents or defense attorneys usually assume responsibility for performing translating or interpreting duties in areas where a specific ethnic minority group is the majority (cf. Chu 2009; Shi 2009; Wu 2009). Yet, it should be noted that most local courts have to face a shortage of qualified bilingual judicial administrators (Shi and Zhao 2012). In places where most inhabitants are Han Chinese or from multiple ethnic minority groups, bilingual students or bilingual teachers of minority origin are usually appointed temporarily to perform translation or interpreting services despite the lack of experience of some of them in terms of law, in translating or interpreting (A'nisha 2009; Cairang 2014).

Due to the underestimation of the demands on high-level translation or interpreting skills and advanced legal knowledge, adequate court translation and interpreting services cannot be guaranteed in many cases, which, as a result, may place obstacles in the way of ethnic linguistic minorities trying to seek fair administration of justice and enjoy their constitutional rights. For example, a defendant who was convicted of theft confessed that he had stolen the accuser's belongings, but he had returned them back to the accuser and had run away after being noticed by the accuser. However, according to the court interpreter, the defendant had stolen the belongings and taken them away after being noticed (Cairang 2014). Under such circumstances, translation policy as a whole fails to reach the goals set by translation management, that is, to provide ethnic linguistic minorities with easier access to justice and enhance their participation in legal affairs. Also, as the rural-to-urban population mobility continues to increase and the demand for translation and interpreting services in the judicial system keeps growing, courts, especially those in areas largely inhabited by Han Chinese, face mounting pressure to ensure that competent translators and interpreters are provided for ethnic linguistic minorities and that available translation and interpreting services provide equal footing to litigants who are not familiar with the language of the court.

In terms of who is expected to translate or interpret in court, views vary from person to person. As a legal expert, Wang (2014) attempts to foster an awareness of the critical role that the court interpreter plays in ensuring ethnic linguistic minorities' access to justice. He suggests that to provide a translation or interpreting service that is balanced and unbiased, bilingual judges should not take dual roles of both trying a case and interpreting, unless interpreters are not able to be present in court due to a natural disaster or other force majeure. As a bilingual judge working for the People's Court of Dong Autonomous County of Hunan Province, Lu (2015) recognizes bilingual judges' roles in enhancing the efficiency of conducting court hearings and providing greater transparency and access to the legal system, but meanwhile, he also points out practical problems in bilingual trials. According to his fieldwork in 50 bilingual trial settings in three local courts, the tasks of court interpreting were taken on by bilingual judges, the parties engaged in lawsuits and even, sometimes, by the audience. This reflects that appreciation of the value of the court interpreter's role in the legal setting is far from being fully developed and some judicial administrators are unaware of the high quality of court translation and interpreting services necessary to bridge the linguistic gap faced by the ethnic linguistic minorities in the judicial proceedings. It is not uncommon that the interpreting causes misunderstanding, which may exacerbate the conflict between the accuser and the accused. Therefore, he holds that to ensure a fair trial and uphold justice, it is critical to improve the legal framework for employing professional court translators and interpreters. Even among citizens, attitudes can be vastly different. In some citizens' eyes, a bilingual judge acts more as a mediator than an interpreter in civil disputes and play an important role in easing the tension by interpreting in a selective way, instead of interpreting everything they said (cf. Shi and Zhao 2012). In contrast, some ethnic linguistic minorities who are engaged in law suits or ethnic audience in court are unsatisfied with bilingual trials and they are skeptical when the bilingual judges shift their languages into Mandarin Chinese to explain something to the Mandarin-speaking party, because they believe that those bilingual judges intend to make it more difficult for them to understand the situation in court by speaking Mandarin Chinese (Lu 2015).

Translating legislative texts

On top of court translation and interpreting, the translation of legislative texts is another instrumental area of work in ensuring equal access to justice. It is mandated that in areas mainly inhabited by a certain ethnic minority group or areas inhabited by a number of ethnic groups, indictments, judgments, notices and other legal documents shall be issued, in the light of actual needs, in the written or spoken language commonly used in the locality (cf. NPC 1979a, article 9; 1979b, article 6; 1984, article 47; 1989, article 9; 1991, article 11). The existence of such articles implicitly requires the translation or interpreting of legislative texts, so as to provide greater transparency and access to the judicial settings. Legal documents written in Mongolian, Tibetan, Uygur, Korean and Kazak can be found on a website named China Judgements Online. However, similar to translation management on court translation and interpreting, legislation on translating legislative texts also lacks clear and standard operating rules for the choice of which minority languages to translate into, who the translator should be, how to translate and what to translate.

Many practices of translating laws have emerged from the practical problems in court translation and interpreting. For instance, to prevent the misunderstandings in court interpreting, the Higher People's Court of Gansu Province has invited professors from several universities as well as bilingual legal experts to edit and translate ten textbooks on the PRC Constitution, Criminal Law of the PRC, Civil Law of the PRC and other national laws into Tibetan language (Wang 2017). This initiative has been approved and supported by the Communist Party of China (CPC) Gansu Provincial Committee and Gansu Provincial Political and Legal Affairs Commission (ibid). Another 23 bilingual textbooks will have been translated and compiled by the end of 2018 (ibid).

Also, due to a shortage of books written in minority languages and a time-consuming process of translating new laws or new commentaries into minority languages (Wu 2009; Shi and Zhao 2012), translators, interpreters and bilingual judicial personnel usually lack a standard work of reference and normative guidelines in their translation practices. In response, work on standardizing and developing legal terms in minority languages has been initiated. For example, a *Hanyu*-Tibetan dictionary of basic legal terms has been translated and edited by the Tibetan Office of Public Prosecution (Zhou 2004a, p. 233). A *Hanyu*-Mongolian dictionary of legal terms has been compiled by the Higher People's Court of Inner Mongolia Autonomous Region (IMAR) and the People's Procuratorate of IMAR. Besides, China Ethnic Languages Translation Bureau has translated several laws and regulations into some minority languages, such as Tibetan, Uyghur, Korean, Mongolian, Kazak and Yi. However, it is worth noting that the number of legislative texts that have been translated into other minority languages is still limited. As a matter of fact, despite having the same legal status, not all ethnic minority groups have the equal opportunity to have translations of legislative texts into their mother tongues. For instance, *Hanyu* (Mandarin Chinese), Dai and Jingpo are co-official languages in Dehong Dai and Jingpo Autonomous Prefecture in Yunnan Province in the southwest of China. However, during the early 1990s, legal documents and announcements released by the prefectural court and the office of public prosecutors were all in *Hanyu* (Zhou 2004b, p. 85).

Translation and interpreting policy: an open and process-related system

From the perspective of complexity theory, translation policy is an "open and process-related" system that is able to "interact with an environment or other systems" (cf. Marais 2015, p. 27, 38). In other words, translation policy as a whole also interacts with other systems (e.g. political policy, economic policy, ethnic policy, educational policy, language policy, etc.). A philosophy of complexity also acknowledges that "the whole" places constraints on its constituent parts (Van Kooten Niekerk and Buhl 2004, p. 4). This insight also applies to translation policy. In different historical, political and social contexts, China's minority language translation policies have been expected by the authority to play different roles, which has prompted translation management, translation practices and translation beliefs to adapt themselves accordingly to the new environment.

When the PRC was established and just started the long-term process of achieving socialism (1949-1957), the government accommodated national differences and embraced multilingualism (Bruhn 2008). In such a political context, translation was valued as a way to ensure minority groups' rights, promote linguistic diversity, and maintain national integrity. China's translation management in this period encouraged multilingualism both nationally and locally. Certain centrally regulated developments were achieved in translation practices (Zhou 2003b; Bruhn 2008).

However, when the government began to expect the arrival of communism (1958-1977), it started adopting an ethnic minority policy and a language policy, which were characterized by assimilationism, so as to stimulate the slow progress of socialism in minority communities (Zhou 2003a, p. 60-61). To foster a monolingual *Hanyu*-only language policy (Zhou 2003a, p. 60) in this political and historical context, translation was disregarded and was even considered as illegal. Articles in the 1954 Constitution concerning the use of local minority languages in government administration and courts were deleted from the 1975 Constitution (Li et al. 2017). This indicates that translation rights were no longer explicitly stipulated by law at that time (ibid). As a result of this translation management, translation practices rarely existed and ethnic minority groups held that learning *Hanyu* was of greater importance and resorting to translation was useless or impossible.

After the Cultural Revolution came to an end, China's policy towards minority languages gradually returned to a policy of accommodation (Zhou 2003a, p. 77; Bruhn 2008). Since the Reform and Opening-up policy was adopted in 1978 and the socialist market economy guidelines were drawn up in 1992, China has witnessed a marked increase in internal rural-to-urban migration. The population mobility has fueled the demand for bridging language gaps through translation and interpreting services and is going to sustain the need for translators and interpreters well into the future. In such a social context, translation policy is supposed to play a role in removing language barriers. Therefore, ethnic linguistic minorities' rights to translation services have been legally guaranteed again since 1982. Efforts have been made to provide translation in the public sphere.

The evolution of China's translation policy shows that in the interactions between translation policy system and other systems, translation policy has been assigned different roles in different contexts. Translation management, translation practices and translation beliefs have changed accordingly to help translation policy to play a certain role. Translation policy keeps evolving out of the interactions with other systems and the interactions among its parts. This means that translation policy is not made all at once. Instead, it is an evolving process, which is consistent with the philosophy shared by complexity theory that reality is "historical" and is "a process of becoming" (Marais 2015, p. 26). Therefore, even when we study current translation policy, it is also necessary to bear in mind that today's components of translation policy might still be under the influence of those in force decades ago. For example, the belief during the *Hanyu* monolingual period that learning *Hanyu* is more important than resorting to translation services is still held by some people these days, which, to some extent, explains the current lack of qualified legal translators and interpreters. Therefore, today's translation practices and translation beliefs, in a way, are still being affected by those which were enacted and accepted in the *Hanyu* monolingual phase (1958–1977).

Concluding remarks

This chapter, through drawing on the cases of China's translation and interpreting policies in the judicial system, has attempted to explore how translation management, translation practices and translation beliefs interact with each other and form translation policy as a whole. Admittedly, systematic, detailed and standard translation management is an essential prerequisite for enabling translation policy to ensure equal access to justice among all the ethnic groups and to promote social integration and national unity. However, only when translation practices and translation beliefs are consistent with translation management, will translation policy play the role that is expected by translation management. This is, as shown in this chapter, not easy to realize mainly because "human beings are not closed systems" (Marais 2015, p. 32). In other words, the same translation management could give rise to distinct interpretations among different individuals and even the same person's thoughts on the same issue may change at different life stages. Consequently, differing translation practices may occur at individual and local levels due to psychological, political, demographic, bureaucratic, economic, and other factors (cf. Bastardas-Boada 2013; Li et al. 2017). Therefore, translation practices and translation beliefs do not always comply with translation management. This partially explains the discrepancies between what has been stipulated by law and what has come true in reality. It also explains why the outcomes of a particular translation policy cannot be predicted.

Further, the social, political and historical contexts in China have forged the role of translation policy in the country and have resulted in the adaptation of the different constituent factors in China's translation policy to different environments. As "a process of becoming," translation policy is an open system that also interacts with other policy systems. It, therefore, calls for an interdisciplinary dynamic approach to adequately apprehend the evolution and emergence of translation policy within certain contexts.

References

A'nisha, 2009. Procedural Justice and Equal Realization of National Languages in Court Trial. *Journal of CUPL*, 3, 44-52, 158-159.

Bastardas-Boada, Albert, 2013. Language Policy and Planning as an Interdisciplinary Field: towards a complexity approach. *Current Issues in Language Planning*, 14(3-4), 363-381.

Bruhn, Daniel, 2008. Minority Language Policy in China, with Observations on the She Ethnic Group, in *Linguistics 250E-Endangered Languages*. Online: http://linguistics.berkeley.edu/~dwbruhn/dwbruhn_250E-paper.pdf.

Cairang, Wangxiu, 2014. The Realization of the Right to Litigating in Ethnic Minority Language: Study on ethnic minority migrants in urban areas. *Guizhou Ethnic Studies*, 3, 14-17.

Cairney, Paul, 2012. Complexity Theory in Political Science and Public Policy. *Political Studies Review*, 10, 346-358.

Chen, Changchun & Liya Liu, 2015. Hanyuan People's Procuratorate Employs Working Staff From the Bureau of the Ethnic and Religious Affairs to Translate and Interpret for Ethnic Minority Groups, *Legal Daily*. Online: http://www.legaldaily.com.cn/locality/content/2015-05/05/content_6070318.htm?node=31019.

Chu, Wanzhong, 2009. The Challenges of Bilingual Litigation in Yunnan Province. *Legal Information*, 4, 48-50.

González Núñez, Gabriel, 2013. Translating for Linguistic Minorities in Northern Ireland: a look at translation policy in the judiciary, healthcare, and local government. *Current Issues in Language Planning*, 14(3-4), 474-489.

———, 2016. *Translating in Linguistically Diverse Societies: Translation Policy in the United Kingdom*. Amsterdam, Philadelphia: John Benjamins.

Guo, Shibao & Jijiao Zhang, 2010. Language, Work, and Learning: Exploring the urban experience of ethnic migrant workers in China. *Diaspora, Indigenous, and Minority Education*, 4(1), 47-63.

Van Kooten Niekerk, Kees & Hans Buhl, 2004. Introduction: comprehending complexity. *In:* Kees Van Kooten Niekerk & Hans Buhl, eds. *The significance of complexity: Approaching a complex world through science, theology and the humanities*. Burlington, VT: Ashgate, 1-18.

Li, Shuang, 2017. Translating for Ethnic Linguistic Minorities: A study on the translation policy in the judicial system in China. *In:* Esther Monzó & Juan Jiménez Salcedo, eds. *Les llengües minoritzades en l'ordre postmonolingüe*. Castelló de la Plana: Universitat Jaume I, 57-69.

Li, Shuang, Duoxiu Qian & Reine Meylaerts, 2017. China's Minority Language Translation Policies (1949-Present). *Perspectives: Studies in Translatology*, 25(4), 540-555.

Liu, Yizhan & Tianwei Wu, 2013. The Ministry of Education of the People's Republic of China: More Than Four Hundred Millions People Are Not Able To Communicate in Mandarin Chinese: Xinhua News Agency. Online: http://www.gov.cn/jrzg/2013-09/05/content_2482016.htm.

Lu, Yinqing, 2015. Procedural Guarantee of Bilingual Trials: Bilingualism at local courts in ethnic minority areas, in *Conference Proceedings for the 26th National Courts Conference*. The 26th National Courts Conference, Beijing, China: Scientific Research Department of National Judges College.

Marais, Kobus, 2015. *Translation Theory and Development Studies: A Complexity Theory Approach*. New York, Abingdon: Routledge.

Meylaerts, Reine, 2011. Translational Justice in a Multilingual World: An Overview of Translational Regimes. *Meta: Journal des traducteurs*, 56(4), 743-757.

———, 2017. Studying Language and Translation Policies in Belgium: What Can We Learn From a Complexity Theory Approach? *Parallèles*, 29(1), 45-59.

Ministry of Education of the People's Republic of China, 2013. *Linguistic Landscape in China*, Beijing. Online: http://www.moe.gov.cn/jyb_sjzl/s5990/201111/t20111114_126551.html.

National Bureau of Statistics of China, 2013. *China Statistical Yearbook 2013*, Beijing: Statistics Press. Online: http://www.stats.gov.cn/tjsj/ndsj/2013/indexeh.htm.

NPC (The National People's Congress), 1979a. Criminal Procedure Law of the PRC. Online: http://www.gov.cn/flfg/2012-03/17/content_2094354.htm.

——— (The National People's Congress), 1979b. Organic Law of the People's Courts of the PRC. Online: http://www.npc.gov.cn/wxzl/gongbao/2006-12/05/content_5354938.htm.

——— (The National People's Congress), 1982. Zhonghua renmin gongheguo xianfa [the Constitution of the People's Republic of China]. Online: www.gov.cn/test/2005-06/14content_6310_3.htm.

——— (The National People's Congress), 1984. Law of the PRC on Regional National Autonomy. Online: http://www.gov.cn/ziliao/flfg/2005-09/12/content_31168.htm.

——— (The National People's Congress), 1989. Administrative Litigation Law of the PRC. Online: http://www.npc.gov.cn/wxzl/gongbao/2014-12/23/content_1892467.htm.

——— (The National People's Congress), 1991. Civil Procedure Law of the PRC. Online: http://www.npc.gov.cn/wxzl/gongbao/2012-11/12/content_1745518.htm.

——— (The National People's Congress), 1997. Criminal Law of the PRC. Online: http://www.npc.gov.cn/huiyi/lfzt/xfxza8/2008-08/21/content_1588538.htm.

NPCSC (The National People's Congress Standing Committee), 2000. The Law of the National Commonly Used Language and Script of the PRC. Online: http://www.gov.cn/ziliao/flfg/2005-08/31/content_27920.htm.

Shi, Wansen, 2009. The Challenges of Translating in Bilingual Litigation. *Legal Information*, 4, 39-43.

Shi, Wansen & Li Zhao, 2012. Bilingual Judges Resolve Disputes in Pastoral Areas, *Legal Daily*. Online: http://www.legaldaily.com.cn/zt/content/2012-11/02/content_3955789.htm?node=40588.

Smuts, Jan Christiaan 1926. *Holism and Evolution*. Westport, Connecticut: Greenwood Press.

Supreme People's Court of the People's Republic of China, 2017. *China's Trials Streaming Site [Zhongguo Tingshen Gongkai Wang]*, Beijing.

Wang, Longwen, 2014. Translation Service System for Ethnic Linguistic Minorities in Court in China. *Chinese Translators Journal*, 3, 68-71.

Wang, Wenjia, 2017. Gansu: Bilingual Trials as the Key to the Judicial System in Ethnic Minority Regions, *People's Daily*. Online: http://www.chinagscourt.gov.cn/detail.htm?id=3677396.

Wu, Yadong, 2009. Bilingual Individuals are Popular Here. *Legal Information*, 4, 43-47.

Zhou, Maocao, 2004a. The Use and Development of Tibetan in China. In: Minglang Zhou & Hongkai Sun, eds. *Language policy in the People's Republic of China: Theory and practice since 1949*. Boston: Kluwer Academic Publishers, 221-237.

Zhou, Minglang, 2003a. *Multilingualism in China: The politics of writing reforms for minority languages 1949–2002*. Berlin: Mouton de Gruyter.

———, 2004b. Minority Language Policy in China: Quality in theory and inequality in practice. In: Minglang Zhou & Hongkai Sun, eds. *Language policy in the People's Republic of China: Theory and practice since 1949*. Boston: Kluwer Academic Publisher, 71–95.

Zhou, Wei, 2003b. Policy Changes with Regard to Tibetan Language - II. China's Tibet, 2, 3–5. *China's Tibet*, 2, 3-5. Online: http://www.cnki.net/kcms/detail/detail.aspx?DbCode=CJFD&dbname=CJFDN7904&filename=ZGXI200302001&uid=WEEvREcwSlJHSldTTGJhYlQ4WTdTcTlhbjF4OW5ZZHpna1pNMEFDQUlobmI=$9A4hF_YAuvQ5obgVAqNKPCYcEjKensW4ggI8Fm4gTkoUKaID8j8gFw!!

Chapter 8

The asymmetry of Canada's language policy regarding access to justice: a model for managing postmonolingualism

Juan Jiménez-Salcedo

Access to justice for official language minorities in Canada has been extensively regulated. The responses given by Canadian legislators, and the interpretations of available statute law made by constitutional judges, have shown differing views on the safeguards to be provided to different types of end-users. This article analyzes the differences between services offered to official language minorities and those made available to allophone communities as reflected both in the legislative arsenal and in the case law. Canadian legislation on bilingualism will be first analyzed before commenting on the wealth of case law resulting from its application. The rights established in both sets of texts will be classified in (a) linguistic rights for speakers of official languages and (b) procedural guarantees for allophones. The discussion of these data will focus on how Canada's judicial institutions have developed models for the management of contemporary postmonolingualism.

Introduction

Access to justice for language minorities in Canada has been extensively regulated. The official bilingualism – French and English – of the Canadian Administration, together with the broad presence of allophone ethnocultural minorities and, to a lesser extent, of indigenous populations, have raised awareness of this postmonolingual context. Such different situations have led to the enactment of legislation on language use in the courtrooms based on the type of end-user. This article analyzes the different decisions taken in facilitating access to criminal justice to users of official minority languages[1] and to members of allophone communities.[2] Legislation establishes that criminal proceedings must take place in the user's language when she or he belongs to the former group; in the latter case, the court may proceed in its habitual language and interpreters are engaged for bridging the language gap between the accused and the court.

The management of languages in the Canadian courtrooms clearly relates to two sets of rights being recognized by different users. The legislative arsenal and the case law resulting from the interpretation of both sets of rights show some disparities. To shed light on the rationale behind such divergences, this article will begin by analyzing Canadian legislation governing bilingualism. The Constitution, then the federal Official Languages Act and the Criminal Code will serve as the basis for elucidating how institutional bilingualism is devised and reflected on the judicial sphere. The wealth of available case law will then clarify how this rule of law has defined, in practice, two different types of rights: linguistic rights for speakers of official languages and procedural guarantees for allophones. The description of this dichotomy will conclude with the presentation of Canada as a country whose judicial institutions are concerned to propose effective models to manage postmonolingualism.

Canada's rule of law with regard to linguistic rights

The right to use either of Canada's two official languages in court proceedings is regulated by a broad raft of legislation. The starting point for the analysis

---

[1] In Canada, an *official language minority* is the linguistic group that speaks the official minority language in the province. All official language minorities in Canada are French-speaking, with the exception of the English-speaking Quebecers. However, they cannot be said to be comparable minorities, since the latter enjoy historic and institutional recognition reflected in the access its members enjoy to services in their own language. Furthermore, minority French-speaking communities are not comparable with one another: hence, the Acadian community of New Brunswick differs substantially from Francophone communities in the West of Canada in terms of demographic weighting and historic recognition.

[2] According to Canadian demolinguistics, the term *allophone* designates a person whose mother tongue is neither French nor English.

conducted here is the Constitution,[3] whose oldest law, the Constitution Act of 1867 (hereinafter, CA 1867), establishes in section 133 (Government of Canada 1867) the freedom to use either of the two official languages in federal or provincial court proceedings.[4]

The Constitution Act of 1870 (Government of Canada 1870) also establishes the freedom for users of courts in the province of Manitoba to choose one of the official languages. Section 19.1 of the Canadian Charter of Rights and Freedoms (hereinafter, the Charter) (Government of Canada 1982) extends this right for citizens of all provinces in the Federation. In spite of the rights-guaranteeing provisions regarding the use of official languages contained in the Constitution, it is interesting to note that legislators did not deem it appropriate to include linguistic discrimination in the list of infringements of human rights articulated in section 15.1 (Campbell 1993-1994, p. 30).

The Official Languages Act (Government of Canada 1985b) fundamentally aims to ensure the advancement of official language communities on equal footing. This Act contains a series of provisions that develop the constitutional guarantees cited above. Hence, section 14 sets out the user's capacity to use French or English at any time during judicial proceedings, as enshrined in the Constitution. Section 15.1 establishes the right to make a statement in the presence of a judge in either of the two official languages, as well as the court's obligation (section 15.2) to provide any interpreting services required in the event that a witness speaks a different official language to that of the parties. Section 15.3 assures the court's power to use interpreting services to assist members of the public attending at a hearing. It should be highlighted in this case that an interpreter is called to mediate because a witness makes use of a different official language to that of the parties. As will be seen later on, judges and district attorneys in criminal proceedings are obliged to use the official language of the accused and are not provided with interpreting services for those languages. The presence or absence of interpreters is key in distinguishing the set of rights given to linguistic minorities in Canadian law.

---

[3] Canada's Constitution is made up of three acts: the Constitution Act of 1867, the Manitoba Act of 1870, and the Constitution Act of 1982. The Constitution Act of 1982 contains a charter of fundamental rights, the Canadian Charter of Rights and Freedoms. Although these acts were passed at politically diverse moments in Canada's history, section 21 of the Charter establishes the impossibility of interpreting the linguistic precepts of this act – the most recent one – in contradiction to the linguistic principles set out by the previous acts (Pelletier 1984, p. 233-234).

[4] The scope of the precept contained in section 133 is specified in ruling of *Quebec v. Blaikie* (Supreme Court of Canada 1979).

Along these same lines, section 16 of the Official Languages Act establishes an obligation for all federal courts to ensure that any trials held under their jurisdiction are presided over by a judge who understands the minority official language of the proceedings, without the intermediation of an interpreter. Supreme Court judges, however, are exempt from this provision, a state of affairs profusely discussed and controverted which has been the subject of a number of legislative bills. At the time of writing this paper, Bill C-203 (House of Commons of Canada 2015) has been defeated at second reading (House of Commons of Canada 2017). Bill C-203 aimed to modify section 5 of the Supreme Court Act (Government of Canada 1985c) to establish the obligation for any judges appointed in the future to understand both official languages (Hudon 2016, p. 13).[5] The different debates held in the Parliament, as well as the opinions published in the press,[6] suggest that the crux of the debate between those in favor and against lies precisely in the intervention of an interpreter. Those in favor of requiring bilingualism on the part of the judges reject the need for intermediation; they also require the linguistic capabilities of Supreme Court judges to be the same as those of bilingual judges in lower chambers.[7] Those against such requirement argue that it is abusive to demand linguistic competences of a judge who is appointed for her extensive knowledge of the Law. Opponents further add that the work of interpreters, who are true specialists in the matter at hand, is an adequate means to compensate for monolingualism on the part of any judges.

In the case of official language minorities, it is the Canadian Criminal Code (Government of Canada 1985a) that sets out the rights of such communities with regard to the courts. Under the Code, criminal courts are bilingual court

---

[5] The bill proposed the addition of a second paragraph to section 5: "In addition, any person referred to in subsection (1) who understands French and English without the assistance of an interpreter may be appointed a judge" (House of Commons of Canada 2015). Note the explicit reference to the absence of an interpreter as proof of the supposed linguistic competency of a judge in both official languages.

[6] Hudon (2016, p. 13-14) establishes an interesting synoptic table on the basis of these sources.

[7] In this regard, note that Bill C-203 is substantially less ambitious, since it only demands an understanding of the official language. Unlike judges from lower jurisdictions in criminal law, the judge would continue to use the language of their choosing. This also occurs today in the case of monolingual French-speaking court judges, who express themselves freely in French during sessions and may be assisted by an interpreter. Detractors of Bill C-203 argue that the imposition of bilingualism would also penalize these judges, since they will no longer be allowed to access interpreting services.

and proceedings must be conducted in the official language of the accused. Section 530(1) establishes that the accused may request[8] the trial to be held in the official language of their choosing. The accused must be informed of the right they have to request the establishment of a specific linguistic regime in their own official language (section 530.3). Section 530.1 guarantees the right of the accused and their lawyer to use either of the two official languages orally during hearings (530.1.a) and in any written documentation submitted to the court (530.1.b). Furthermore, the judge and the attorney must speak in the language of the accused during the trial (530.1.d and 530.1.e). That same language must be used by the court in providing the accused with the records of proceedings during the preliminary inquiry and trial (530.1.g), and with the full judgement at the end of the proceedings (530.1.h).[9]

Case law on linguistic rights:
from the restrictive interpretation of the law to the *Beaulac* judgement

It might seem that the right to make use of an official language in court is clearly defined in light of the Criminal Code. However, this right has been subject to unstable interpretative case-law since the 1980s. This is undoubtedly due to the difficulty of harmonizing the linguistic rights of the accused with the administrative functioning of the courts, and even with the linguistic rights of judicial staff, chiefly judges and attorneys. Furthermore, case law reflects existing difficulties defining whether the right to use an official language is a linguistic right – with the resulting consequences in terms of recognition of the Federation's national communities –, or whether it is a procedural right.

The distinction between the two types of rights has important consequences in the sphere under examination, since linguistic rights are grounded in the creation of institutionally bilingual courts, whereas the need to assure procedural guarantees is resolved through the intervention of an interpreter. This differentiation was gradually enshrined in case law, particularly following *Beaulac* judgement (Supreme Court of Canada 1999). It

---

[8] The timeframes within which the accused may request the institution of a bilingual court are established in paragraphs a, b and c of section 530.1, and vary according to the nature of proceedings. Even so, section 530.4 of this instrument also allows for an extraordinary procedure to request the language of the trial to be changed outside of this period. There is even the possibility of asking for the trial to be held in both official languages, by virtue of the provisions set out in section 530.5.

[9] This right to have access to criminal trial documentation in the official language of the accused extends to all documentation of the proceedings, including forms, as set out under section 849.3 of this same act.

is interesting to note how this has become the subject for debate, since, as Justice Dickson indicates (Supreme Court of Canada 1986c, p. paragraph 27), both rights could overlap insofar as the fulfillment of the accused's rights depends on the existence of effective communication. This perspective is shared by part of the literature (Braën 1998), which considers that, although it is not part of the block of linguistic rights, the right to an interpreter can exercise a certain influence over linguistic rights.

Beyond these particular considerations, the doctrine established definitively by case law has been that of a clear separation between linguistic rights and procedural guarantees, which results in the intervention of an interpreter when the accused is an allophone, a right enshrined in section 14 of the Charter (Government of Canada 1982) and sufficiently interpreted in case law, as we shall see later on. If the Canadian body of laws is compared with that of other Western countries, the inclusion of this provision in the Constitution is exceptional. Section 14 is part of the block that sets out procedural guarantees, separate from the sections consolidating linguistic rights. Having said this, the separation between the two rights could imply a certain hierarchical organization, since direct access to an essential service, such as the judiciary, directly and without the need for an interpreter, guarantees a degree of protection for language communities that is missing from the merely procedural protection that assures the right to an interpreter.[10]

This is undoubtedly the interpretation that could be derived from the aforementioned distinction from the perspective of Law. From a more sociopolitical point of view, it should not be forgotten that the free use of one's own language in a court of law reflects a certain conception of language policy. This might respond, once again, to the distinction introduced by Canada's legislators between official language communities and allophone communities, and the consequence this has in terms of the generation of rights in access to public services. The legislators could be accused of establishing a hierarchy with regard to the direct access available to an official language speaker over an allophone. The concept of allophone – so widely used in Canada – could even be criticized, as a kind of reification of ethnocultural categories such as "non-Canadian," "non-French-speaking" or

---

[10] Regarding the proposed bill to modify the Supreme Court Act (House of Commons of Canada 2015), it could be said that the discourse of those in favor of bilingual judges indicates a certain prejudice concerning the type of communication guaranteed by an interpreter. Even though the figure of the interpreter is broadly accepted in the Canadian context, some may still hold a perception of communication mediated by an interpreter as being necessarily of lower quality.

"non-English-speaking." However, the Canadian public service context is not very different from that of the majority of Western countries, in which the recognition of ethnocultural communities is usually fairly limited. This being said, the efforts undertaken by various Canadian judicial institutions to ensure access to justice under equal conditions should also be highlighted.[11]

It could be said that the doctrinal distinction between linguistic rights and procedural guarantees has been enshrined ever since the *Beaulac* judgement. Case law did not automatically adopt the distinction, but instead underwent a series of ups and downs over the course of the 1980s and 90s.

An initial group of judgements in the 90s issued by the Superior Court of Quebec pertain to the language used by the attorney during oral proceedings. In *R. v. Cross* (Superior Court of Quebec 1993), it was deemed that the provisions of section 530.1.e of the Criminal Code were not applicable in Quebec courtrooms, since there was a contradiction between the accused's rights acknowledged in the Code and the requirements of section 133 CA 1867, by virtue of which the district attorney could address the judge at any time in French, and the judge could not oppose this. However, in *R. v. Montour* (Superior Court of Quebec 1991), the full constitutionality of the provisions set out in the Criminal Code was affirmed. The doctrine was subsequently unified in the judgement of *Cross v. Teasdale* (Quebec Court of Appeal 1998). The court established that, once the accused's request has been approved by the court, it is the responsibility of the attorney's office to provide an attorney for that case capable of understanding and speaking the official language of the proceedings and who agrees to intervene in the trial only in that language. Hence, the judgement summarizes two linguistic rights: those of the attorney, a representative of a bilingual institution, and those of the accused, contained in the Criminal Code as a reflection of principles enshrined in the Constitution (Braën 1998, p. 393).

Another group of judicial rulings encompassed the three decisions known as the "1986 trilogy" (Doucet 2011, p. 286-287), so called because the three were issued in that same year: *Société des Acadiens du Nouveau-Brunswick Inc. v. Association of Parents for Fairness in Education* (Supreme Court of Canada 1986c), *MacDonald v. City of Montreal* (Supreme Court of Canada 1986b) and *Bilodeau v. Manitoba (Att. Gen.)* (Supreme Court of Canada 1986a). In spite of prior recognition of the equality of official languages by case law pertaining to section 133 CA 1867, these three judgements enshrined

---

[11] For a specific analysis of the media of interpretation, as well as the adoption of specific quality criteria in the Montreal Court House and in Canadian administrative justice, see Jiménez-Salcedo (2010, p. 177-199).

a restrictive interpretation of rights linked to official languages in the judicial sphere (Braën 1998, p. 388).

The restrictive vision of the 1986 trilogy is grounded in the consideration of linguistic rights as political rights and not as fundamental rights. The *MacDonald* ruling made it clear that, although it was undeniable that users of judicial services could address them in any of the two official languages, it was also true that neither CA 1867 nor the Charter establish any obligation requiring these services to respond to the user in that language. Equally, in *Société des Acadiens* the Court interpreted section 19.2 of the Charter as permitting citizens of the province of New Brunswick to litigate in French, although it similarly does not impose an obligation upon the judge to know or speak that language. The judges, in this case, reached a minimalist interpretation of section 19.2 and, hence, of section 133 CA 1867, since they understood that the legislator did not impose an obligation on judicial staff to know, be competent, or even to understand the official language that the user was at full liberty to use.

In this context, it was up to the political powers to bestow upon official languages a broader place in the judicial sphere, since the scope of official languages in courts was classed within the realm of political rights. The goal of progressing the two official languages established by section 16.3 of the Charter links federal parliament and provincial parliaments, responsible for giving content to the provisions of the Charter. According to the doctrine of the Supreme Court, courts cannot be expected to perform political functions (Braën 1998, p. 390-391). By limiting the scope of linguistic rights, the effective freedom of use of official languages would only be safeguarded by the procedural guarantees inscribed in other sections of the Charter (Campbell 1993-1994, p. 57-58). This restrictive vision of legislation was particularly discriminatory with regard to French.[12]

Finally, the *R. v. Beaulac* ruling (Supreme Court of Canada 1999) ushered in a doctrinal U-turn with regard to linguistic rights. *Beaulac* enshrined the difference between linguistic and procedural rights and extolled a broader and more generous interpretation of these rights. It fulfilled the principles of equality between the two language communities expressed in the Constitution and, above all, in the application of the right to be judged in the official language of their choosing as long as the request is made sufficiently in advance so that the material and human resources can be made available.

---

[12] French is official throughout the Federation but has a very limited presence in certain communities outside of the bilingual belt that encompasses the provinces of Ontario, Quebec and New Brunswick.

The asymmetry of Canada's language policy

According to *Beaulac*, the right to choose the official language of judicial proceedings is not a procedural guarantee. In the opinion of the ruling judge, Justice Bastarache, it is a binding right for public powers, which must provide the necessary material and human resources to allow bilingual courts to be constituted. The absence of these resources cannot be cited as justification not to accede to the request of the accused party made by virtue of section 530 of the Criminal Code. As established by point 39 of the ruling, these are not compensatory measures – as the intervention of an interpreter might be – put in place by a monolingual court that must accommodate a request for a bilingual trial. According to this ruling, the judicial system must adapt to the linguistic needs of the accused. The use of one or the other official language must not be interpreted, according to the Supreme Court, exclusively in terms of judicial equity, but should respond to the expression of the linguistic and cultural identity of the accused, who is above all a user of a public service.

Intervention of an interpreter as a procedural guarantee

As indicated previously, if the accused does not speak either of Canada's two official languages – or if she or he is not considered sufficiently competent to use them in court – their right to access justice is safeguarded by the provisions of section 14 of the Charter (Government of Canada 1982). The court does not adapt to the language of the accused, as in the case of official-language speakers; instead, a compensatory measure is implemented.

It is interesting to see how judges have been able to delve into matters related with the work of interpreters in case law regarding the provisions of section 14; for example, regarding the quality of interpreting services provided in courtrooms. In 1973, *R. v. Reale* (Court of Appeal for Ontario 1973), confirmed in 1975 (Supreme Court of Canada 1975), explained how the principles of continuity[13] and concomitance[14] were essential in order to provide quality interpreting services in criminal justice. These quality criteria have conditioned the interpreting techniques used in the courtrooms. It should also be underlined that these quality indicators have been established on the basis of legal criteria, since only continuity and concomitance can assure that procedural guarantees are safeguarded. One decade after *Reale*, the *Hertrich* (Court of Appeal for Ontario 1982) judgement issued by that same court coincided with these criteria and underscored the absolute need

---

[13] Interpreting should be provided without interruption.
[14] Interpreting should be formulated as discourse is produced in the language that the accused party does not understand.

for the continual presence of the interpreter throughout the entire proceedings.[15]

However, the decision that enshrines the major principles of quality in judicial interpreting is undoubtedly *R. v. Tran* (Supreme Court of Canada 1994). As in previous case law, the argument in favor of the intervention of an interpreter is formulated in accordance with the provisions set out in the Charter for procedural matters. Furthermore, the ruling refers not only to section 14 but also to sections 15 (equality) and 27 (aspiration of the Canadian people to become a multicultural society), thus explaining in terms of political philosophy the importance attached to the figure of the interpreter in criminal proceedings. In *Tran*, the principles of quality set out in the *Reale* judgement are expanded upon, since the principles of fidelity and impartiality are added to those of continuity and concomitance. The question of fidelity is always complex within the sphere of legal interpreting, since the interpreter might be inclined to go beyond the minimalist interpretation represented by a literal translation of discourse and provide a more explanatory mediation. Some authors (Deferrari 1989, p. 126; Noreau 2003, p. 197) extoll the need to avoid explanatory interpretations, since it is not the interpreter's role to compensate for a lack of clarity on the part of certain judicial staff.

These principles were formulated in response to the appeal lodged with the Court in the case of *Tran*. The decision handed down by the lower court was reproached for the fact that the accused did not have a continuous interpreting service throughout the hearing and, therefore, the principles of continuity and concomitancy were not respected. The Supreme Court also advocates fidelity, since the accused only had access to a translation of an excerpt from the declaration of the prosecution witness. Impartiality is incorporated into the judgement precisely because this witness had acted as his own interpreter, translating his own testimony. Although the solutions thought up ad hoc by the lower court to resolve the language gap were bordering on the absurd, and therefore the Court had more than enough arguments to reverse the previous ruling, the major principles of quality expressed in *Tran* are applicable to any language interpreting within criminal legal proceedings, and should, of course, be taken into account beyond the Canadian borders.

---

[15] The criterion of continuity is broadly described in subsequent case law: *R. v. Petrovic* (Court of Appeal for Ontario 1984), *Tung v. Canada* (Federal Court of Appeal 1991) and, especially in *R. v. Tran* (Supreme Court of Canada 1994).

Conclusion

The management of languages in Canadian courts is a good reflection of how to move beyond the monolingual ideology that still dominates many administrative services, in Western countries at any rate. In the case of Canada, recognition of this postmonolingualism is varied. It has generated case law that reflects the existing social and political debate about the role of languages in a multicultural democracy.

The language policy developed in accordance with this postmonolingual age is asymmetrical on account of the very complexity of the phenomenon they seek to order. In his proposal of a multicultural model for Canada, Kymlicka (1998) establishes hierarchies between national minorities and ethnocultural groups. The holding of bilingual trials, applying the broad interpretation of section 530 of the Criminal Code given in *Beaulac*, is subject to control and vigilance, since French in Canada is still a minoritized language, even in Quebec. In the case of French, the reasoning given by the legislator and its judicial interpretation is very simple: it is not acceptable for Canadian citizens to be discriminated against in their own country on account of the language they use in a court of law. That guarantee of non-discrimination is extended in practice not only to people with Canadian citizenship, but to those who have decided to make French their language of identification on Canadian soil. In a postmonolingual context such as that of Canada, this implies recognizing membership of an organic citizenship defined by means of linguistic uses.

With regard to interpreters and their intervention in the name of the procedural guarantees, the fulfillment of quality criteria, expressed in case law itself, undoubtedly entails moving beyond the vision of the interpreter as a burdensome presence in a courtroom accustomed to working monolingually (Wadensjö 1997, p. 36). The assumption of these criteria by judicial authorities themselves should serve, beyond the Canadian context, to normalize the presence of interpreters in the courtroom and, therefore, to give greater visibility to the postmonolingualism inherent in multiculturalism.

References

Braën, André, 1998. L'interprétation judiciaire des droits linguistiques au Canada et l'affaire Beaulac. *Revue générale de droit*, 29(4), 379-409.

Campbell, Gordon Scott, 1993-1994. Language, Equality and the Charter: Collective Versus Individual Rights in Canada and Beyond. *National Journal of Constitutional Law*, 4(1), 29-73.

Court of Appeal for Ontario, 1973. R. v. Reale, 13 CCC (2d), 345.

———, 1982. R. v. Hertrich, 67 CCC (2d), 510.

———, 1984. R. v. Petrovic, 13 CCC (3d), 416.

Deferrari, Matilde, 1989. Judiciary Interpretation: Theory and Practice. *In:* Deanna Lindberg Hammond, ed. *Coming of Age. Proceedings of the 30th Annual Conference of the American Translators Association.* Washington D.C., Medford (NJ): Learned Information, 123-127.

Doucet, Michel, 2011. La Cour suprême du Canada et le principe de la progression vers l'égalité des droits linguistiques : un dialogue inachevé ? *In:* Nicolas Lambert, ed. *À l'avant-garde de la dualité. Mélanges en l'honneur de Michel Bastarache.* Cowansville: Yvon Blais, 281-322.

Federal Court of Appeal, 1991. Tung v. Canada (Minister of Employment and Immigration), 124 NR, 388.

Government of Canada, 1867. Constitution Act. Online: http://laws-lois.justice.gc.ca/eng/Const/page-1.html.

———, 1870. Manitoba Act. Online: http://www.justice.gc.ca/eng/rp-pr/csj-sjc/constitution/lawreg-loireg/p1t21.html.

———, 1982. Constitution Act / Canadian Charter of Rights and Freedoms. Online: http://laws-lois.justice.gc.ca/eng/Const/page-15.html.

———, 1985a. Criminal Code. Online: http://laws-lois.justice.gc.ca/eng/acts/C-46/.

———, 1985b. Official Languages Act. Online: http://laws-lois.justice.gc.ca/eng/acts/O-3.01/.

———, 1985c. Supreme Court Act. Online: http://laws-lois.justice.gc.ca/eng/acts/S-26/.

House of Commons of Canada, 2015. Supreme Court Act, Bill C-203. Online: http://www.parl.ca/DocumentViewer/en/42-1/bill/C-203/first-reading/page-4.

———, 2017. Vote no. 374, Sitting no. 222, Bill C-203. Online: https://www.ourcommons.ca/Parliamentarians/en/votes/42/1/374.

Hudon, Marie-Ève, 2016. *Le bilinguisme dans les tribunaux fédéraux.* Ottawa: Bibliothèque du Parlement.

Jiménez Salcedo, Juan, 2010. *Traducción-interpretación en los servicios públicos en Quebec: ¿un modelo para Andalucía?* Seville: Centro de Estudios Andaluces.

Kymlicka, Will, 1998. *Finding Our Way. Rethinking Ethnocultural Relations in Canada.* New York: Oxford University Press.

Noreau, Pierre, 2003. *Le droit en partage: le monde juridique face à la diversité ethnoculturelle.* Montréal: Éditions Thémis.

Pelletier, Benoît, 1984. Les pouvoirs de légiférer en matière de langue après la Loi constitutionnelle de 1982. *Les Cahiers de droit,* 25(1), 227-297.

Quebec Court of Appeal, 1998. Cross v. Teasdale, RJQ, 2587.

Superior Court of Quebec, 1991. R. v. Montour, RJQ, 1470.

———, 1993. R. v. Cross, 76 CCC (3d), 445.

Supreme Court of Canada, 1975. Ontario (Att. Gen.) v. Reale, 2 SCR, 624.

———, 1979. Québec (Att. Gen.) v. Blaikie et al., 2 SCR, 1016. Online: https://scc-csc.lexum.com/scc-csc/scc-csc/en/item/2637/index.do.

———, 1986a. Bilodeau v. Manitoba (Att. Gen.), 1 SCR, 449. Online: https://scc-csc.lexum.com/scc-csc/scc-csc/en/item/136/index.do.

———, 1986b. MacDonald v. Ville de Montréal, 1 SCR, 460. Online: https://scc-csc.lexum.com/scc-csc/scc-csc/en/item/137/index.do.

———, 1986c. Société des Acadiens du Nouveau-Brunswick Inc. v. Association of Parents for Fairness in Education, 1 SCR, 549. Online: https://scc-csc.lexum.com/scc-csc/scc-csc/en/item/138/index.do.

———, 1994. R. v. Tran, 2 SCR, 951. Online: https://scc-csc.lexum.com/scc-csc/scc-csc/en/item/1166/index.do.

———, 1999. R. v. Beaulac, 1 SCR, 768. Online: https://scc-csc.lexum.com/scc-csc/scc-csc/en/item/1700/index.do.

Wadensjö, Cecilia, 1997. Recycled information as a questioning strategy. Pitfall in interpreted-mediated talk. *In:* Silvana E. Carr, R. P. Roberts, A. Dufour & D. Steyn, eds. *The Critical Link: Interpreters in the Community.* Amsterdam: John Benjamins Publishing, 35-52.

List of contributors

Esther Monzó-Nebot is an Associate Professor at the Translation and Communication Studies Department of Universitat Jaume I, where she is the director of the Master's Program in Translation and Interpreting Research, coordinates the research group "Translation and Postmonolingualism" (TRAP), and the legal and administrative language section of Revista de Llengua i Dret / Journal of Language and Law. She is a member of the Research Institute in Feminist and Gender Studies and of the Research Institute in Valencian Philology. Between 2013 and 2015 she was a Professor at the Translation and Interpreting Studies Department of the University of Graz, Austria. She has been a practicing translator at the United Nations, the World Trade Organization and the World Intellectual Property Organization. She has published on the sociological and textual aspects of legal and institutional translation and interpreting, computer-aided translation and translation and interpreting training. Her current research focuses on the psychosocial aspects of translation and interpreting.

Gernot Hebenstreit holds a doctoral degree in translation studies and is working as a senior researcher at the Institute of Translation Studies at the University of Graz, Austria. He is a member of the technical committee on Terminology and Language Resources at the Austrian Standards Institute and of ISO TC 37. His areas of teaching comprise translation theory, translation ethics, terminology theory and management, information technologies and translation. His research interests include translation theory, terminology of translation studies, translation ethics, multimodal translation, terminology theory, terminological analysis and modeling of concepts and conceptual structures.

Juan Jiménez-Salcedo is an Associate Professor at the Department of Translation and Philology at Pablo de Olavide University (Seville, Spain), where he co-directs the Research Seminar on Gender and Cultural Studies. He holds a PhD in Humanities from François Rabelais University in Tours (France) and a PhD in French Language and Literature from the Basque Country University (Spain). He taught at the University of France-Comté (France) between 2005 and 2007. In 2009 he was a post-doctoral researcher at the Centre for Ethnic Studies at the University of Montreal (Canada) and in 2017 was a Visiting Professor at the University of Mons (Belgium). His recent research interests lie in the fields of interpreting in public services (primarily in the courts), language policies in Canada and Catalan-speaking territories, French-Catalan and French-Spanish legal translation, and legal and administrative drafting in these languages.

Luis Andrade Ciudad is an Assistant Professor at the Pontificia Universidad Católica del Perú, Peru. His research focuses on Andean linguistics and language contact.

M. Rosario Martín Ruano (GIR Traducción, Ideología, Cultura) teaches translation at the University of Salamanca. Her research interests include legal and institutional translation, translation theory, gender studies and postcolonial critique. She has published several books, anthologies and essays on these issues, including *El (des)orden de los discursos: la traducción de lo políticamente correcto* (2003, Granada: Comares), *Translation and the Construction of Identity* (2005, Seoul: IATIS, co-edited with Juliane House and Nicole Baumgarten), *Traducción, política(s), conflictos: legados y retos para la era del multiculturalismo* (2013, Granada: Comares, co-edited with María Carmen África Vidal Claramonte), and *Traducción, medios de comunicación, opinión pública* (2016, Granada: Comares, co-edited with María Carmen África Vidal Claramonte). She is also a practicing translator.

Michael Cronin is Professor of French (1776) at Trinity College Dublin. He received his BA from Trinity College Dublin, his MA from University College Dublin and his PhD from Trinity College Dublin. He taught in the Université of Tours, the École Normale Supéreiure (Cachan) and was Director of the Centre for Translation and Textual Studies at Dublin City University. He is an elected Member of the Royal Irish Academy, the Academia Europaea and is an Officer in the Ordre des Palmes Académiques. His research interests cover a wide range of topics and currently focus on developing eco-criticism in relation to modern languages and translation, exploring the notion of 'translation trauma' in relation to population displacement and investigating language identities as mediated through travel.

Raquel de Pedro Ricoy holds a PhD in Arts (Translation) from the University of Edinburgh and is Chair of Translation and Interpreting at the University of Stirling, UK. Previously, she was an Associate Professor at Heriot-Watt University, UK, and has also worked as a freelance translator and interpreter. Her current research interests focus on the sociocultural dimensions of translation and interpreting, and the role of both these activities in public-service delivery, especially in post-colonial contexts.

Rosaleen Howard is Chair of Hispanic Studies in the School of Modern Languages at Newcastle University, UK. She was previously Senior Lecturer at the Institute of Latin American Studies, University of Liverpool, UK. Her research focuses on the Quechua language, linguistic anthropology and sociolinguistics of the Andes. She has published widely on Quechua storytelling and oral history; anthropological approaches to the study of language contact, especially translation issues; language politics and cultural identity in the Andes; and intercultural education policy for indigenous peoples.

Shuang Li is a PhD candidate in the Translation Studies Research Unit of the Faculty of Arts at KU Leuven. She is currently a PhD candidate and works on China's current translation policies towards minority languages under the supervision of Prof. Dr. Reine Meylaerts. With Duoxiu Qian and Reine Meylaerts, she has published papers on this topic (in *Perspectives*, with Duoxiu Qian and Reine Meylaerts and in a collective volume edited by E. Monzó and J. Jiménez). She has regularly presented her work on China's translation policy at international academic conferences.

Index

A

animal species, 88
Anthropocene, 85
assimilationism, 11
Australia, 81

B

Babel, 11, 12, 24
  Tower of Babel, 10, 14
Bagua trials, 94, 95, 97, 100, 101, 102, 103, 104
bias
  categorical bias, 18
  cognitive bias, 9, 17, 23
  confirmation bias, 4, 20
  evaluative bias, 17
  ingroup affinity, 17
  intergroup hostility, 4, 18, 20, 21
  intragroup affinity, 4
  prejudice, 4, 17, 18, 23
bilingualism, 127, 128, 130
  institutional bilingualism, 128, 130, 131, 133
Bourdieu, Pierre, 49, 65

C

Canada, 127–37
carbon emissions, 79
Chesterman, Andrew, 68, 69, 70, 71
China, 111
climate change, 79, 80, 85
cognitive biases. *See* bias
colonialism, 93
colonization, 78, 85
complexity theory, 114, 121, 122
conflict
  intergroup conflict, 5, 18, 19, 24
  intergroup hate, 20, 21
  minimization of conflict, 68
  violence, 53
consensus, 68
contact hypothesis, 19
  extended contact hypothesis, 19
cooperation, 10, 12, 15, 21
  intergroup cooperation, 16

D

deep history, 85
democracy, 80, 137
  democratic culture, 66
  ethnolinguistic democracy, 36
development, 79
dialogue, 68
difference, 10, 36, 45, 48, 53, 87
diglossia, 38
  code-blending, 38
  language intertwining, 38
  scode-switching, 38
discrimination, 11, 13, 21
  linguistic discrimination, 129, 137
disempowerment, 11
diversity, 9, 10, 12, 13, 14, 16, 19, 20, 22, 37, 39, 41
  diversity intelligence, 23
Downward Comparison Theory, 18

E

ecolinguistics, 78

ecology, 79
ecosystem, 80
Edelman, Murray, 19
energy sources, 78
environmental impact, 80
equality, 80
equality of opportunities, 68
ethical principles
   clarity, 68
   cooperativeness, 66, 70, 71
   courage, 70
   determination, 70
   ecologicality, 66, 70, 71
   empathy, 69
   fairness, 69
   honesty, 69
   loyalty, 66, 70, 71
   transparency, 66, 70, 71
   trust, 68
   truth, 68
   truthfulness, 69
   understanding, 68, 70
ethics, 9, 61
   translation ethics, 88
   virtue ethics, 67, 69
ethnicity, 11
   ethnic groups, 12, 16, 111, 112, 115, 118, 120, 121, 122
      ethnic linguistic minorities, 113, 114, 116, 117, 119, 122
      Han, 111
   ethnic linguistic minorities, 111
EU. *See* European Union
European Union, 36, 39, 42, 46, 48, 49
excellence, 69
extinction, 88

F

fidelity, 136
fossil fuels, 78, 80

freedom, 63, 68, 134
functionalist Translation Studies, 65

G

gender, 107
globalization, 69
Great Britain, 83

H

Hanyu. See Mandarin Chinese
heritage, 9, 10, 11
Hieronymic oath, 72
Honduras, 79
human dignity, 68
human exceptionalism, 87
human rights, 47, 68, 79, 129

I

identity, 39, 53
   social identity, 3, 16, 19
      identity threat, 21
ideology, 44, 53, 61, 63
impartiality, 46
inclusivity, 36
indigenous cultures, 78
indigenous peoples, 79
information processing, 17
institutions, 3
   educational institutions, 3
   judicial institutions, 4, 128
   police, 4
intergroup relations, 23
international organizations, 47, 49, 52
interpreting. *See* translation and interpreting

Index

J

justice, 9, 41, 45, 68, 80, 81, 82, 86, 87, 88
  access to justice, 91, 93, 106, 107, 112, 116, 117, 119, 123, 127, 128, 130, 131, 132, 133, 135
  administration of justice, 116, 117
  climate justice, 79, 80, 81, 82, 85, 87, 89
  criminal justice, 128
  criminal proceedings, 129
  environmental justice, 79, 86
  hermeneutical injustice, 45
  intercultural justice, 95
  procedural guarantees, 127, 128
  social justice, 3, 25, 43

L

language rights, 92, 94, 107, 112, 127, 128, 132, 128–35
  access to political rights, 111
  access to public services, 112
  access to social rights, 111
  access to T&I, 113, 119, 130, 131, 132, 135–36
  assimilationism, 122
  linguistic diversity, 122
  right to interpreting, 92, 93
  right to T&I, 122
  right to translation, 93, 95
  right to translation and interpreting, 97
language teaching, 82
languages
  Anglo-Romani, 83
  Aymara, 105
  Cornish, 83
  Doric, 83
  endangered languages, 82
  English, 35, 40, 46, 50, 51, 54, 55, 82, 83, 127, 128, 129
  English dialects, 83, 84
  French, 46, 50, 51, 54, 127, 128, 129, 130, 133, 134, 137
  Gaelic, 83
  German, 46
  indigenous languages, 81, 92, 93, 97, 106, 111
  Irish, 83
  Jaru, 81
  Kazak, 120
  Kija, 81
  Korean, 120
  Kriol, 81
  lesser-used languages, 78
  lingua franca, 11, 40, 92
  major languages, 82
  Mandarin Chinese, 112, 120, 121, 122, 123
  minoritized languages, 80, 81, 88, 91, 120, 121, 137
  minoritized major languages, 85
  minority languages, 44, 78, 81, 83, 84, 122
  minority official languages, 130
  Mongolian, 120
  Native American languages, 78
  Norman, 83
  Norn and Old English, 83
  official languages, 36, 127, 128, 129, 130, 131, 134
  official minority language, 128
  Orcadian, 83
  Polish, 48
  Quechua, 105
  Scots Gaelic, 84
  Shetlandic, 83
  Spanish, 37, 51, 92, 93, 96, 97, 100, 102, 103, 105, 106
  Tibetan, 116, 120, 121

Uygut, 120
Welsh, 83
League of Nations, 88
legislation, 127
linguistic legislation, 128
linguistic policies
    language policy, 62, 92, 113, 127, 132
    translation policy, 36, 42, 82, 113, 114, 121, 122, 123
liquid modernity, 25
liquid nature, 79
literary studies, 87

M

manipulative elite hypothesis, 21
Manitoba, 129
melting pot, 11
minorities. *See* social groups
minoritization, 82, 85
misrecognition, 46
monolingualism, 3, 9, 38, 42, 102, 122, 123, 130, 137
moral virtues, 67, 69
multiculturalism, 12, 14, 15, 35, 137
multilingualism, 9, 11, 35, 36, 37, 38, 39, 42, 46, 93, 111, 116, 122
    borrowing, 38
    code-alternation, 38
    codemeshing, 38
    code-mixing, 38
    crossing, 38
    heteroglossia, 38
    languaging, 38
    metrolingualism, 38
    nonce-borrowing, 38
    polylanguaging, 38
    translanguaging, 38
myths, 9, 10, 12, 19, 20, 21
myth-symbol complex, 19

N

narratives, 19, 20, 35
neutrality, 61

O

Oakeshott, Michael, 14
otherness, 9, 10, 11, 12, 14, 15, 16, 17, 18, 22, 24, 68

P

Peru, 92–107
Peruvian State. *See* Peru
pluralism, 37
plurilingualism, 38, 39, 81
policymakers, 13
political systems
    democracy, 3, 9, 12, 13, 14
    populist majoritarianism, 2, 25
postmonolingualism, 9, 13, 127, 128, 137
power, 4, 10, 11, 49, 61, 78, 79
prestige, 38
privilege, 3, 14
procedural languages, 46
professionalism, 62, 68, 70
Prunč, Erich, 61, 64–66, 72

Q

Quebec, 137

R

Rawls, John, 3, 13, 25
recognition, 41, 42, 47, 53, 55
redistribution, 41
representation, 87
resilience, 80
resources, economical use of, 68
respect, 68

rule of law, 128

S

sameness, 12, 14, 36, 45, 47, 49
Scanlon, Thomas Michael, 15
Sen, Amartya, 14, 15
social groups, 17
 allophone communities, 7, 127, 128, 132
 ethnocultural minorities, 127
 indigenous populations, 127
 ingroup, 16, 17, 18, 19, 20, 21
 intergroup relations, 2, 9, 17
 language minorities, 127, 129
 minorities, 68
 minorities', 21
 official language communities, 129, 132
 official language minorities, 127, 128, 130
 official language minority, 128
 outgroup, 12, 18, 20, 21
social justice. *See* justice
solidarity, 68
South Africa, 55
Spain, 48
status, 66
super-diversity, 39
sustainability, 68, 72, 80
symbolic politics, 19
symbolic violence, 35, 46

T

terminology, 101
Tibet, 116
tolerance, 68
Tower of Babel. *See* Babel
transitology, 80
translation. *See* translation and interpreting

translation and interpreting, 9, 11, 23, 35, 36, 37, 78, 80, 81, 82, 87
 ad hoc interpreting, 91, 93
 bilingual T&I, 118, 119
 community interpreting, 96
 court interpreting, 106, 128, 129, 130, 131, 135
 court T&I, 117, 119
 interpreting techniques, 135
 intersemiotic translation, 88
 language brokering, 95, 96
 legal and institutional translation, 39, 40, 41, 42, 46, 49, 55
 legislation on T&I, 117
 qualified T&I, 123
 role, 9, 37, 62, 63, 93
 role expectations, 103, 107
 T&I certification, 117
 T&I ethics, 96, 98, 107, 117
 T&I neutrality, 98
 T&I quality, 118
 T&I training, 95, 106
 translation of legislative texts, 120
 translation zone, 81
 translation/interpreting culture, 72
Translation and Interpreting Studies, 12, 17, 80, 88
Translation Studies. *See* Translation and Interpreting Studies
Translationskultur. *See* 'translation/interpreting culture'

U

understanding, 11, 12, 16, 17, 22, 23, 24, 49
United Nations, 2, 20, 49

V

values, 16, 17, 20, 80
   value theory, 67
virtue ethics. *See* ethics

W

worldview, 46

www.ingramcontent.com/pod-product-compliance
Lightning Source LLC
Chambersburg PA
CBHW061842300426
44115CB00013B/2482